# TREASURES
# OF
# TUTANKHAMUN

BALLANTINE BOOKS • NEW YORK

*The photograph at the right shows a tiny wreath of fresh leaves and petals that had been placed around the royal symbols on Tutankhamun's outermost coffin*

*The drawings on the first and last pages represent cartouches containing hieroglyphic signs that render Tutankhamun's personal name with his usual epithet, "Tutankhamun, ruler of On of Upper Egypt [a name for Thebes]," and his throne name, "Nebkheperura"*

This is the catalogue for an exhibition lent between 1976 and 1979 by the Cairo Museum to the National Gallery of Art, Field Museum of Natural History and the Oriental Institute of The University of Chicago, New Orleans Museum of Art, Los Angeles County Museum of Art, Seattle Art Museum, and The Metropolitan Museum of Art. The exhibition was made possible by generous gifts from Exxon Corporation and the Robert Wood Johnson Jr. Charitable Trust, matched by grants from the National Endowment for the Humanities.

The color photographs, made especially for this exhibition, were taken in Cairo by Lee Boltin, with Ken Kay.

Most of the black and white pictures were made in the course of Howard Carter's excavation of Tutankhamun's tomb by the expedition photographer, Harry Burton. Prints were made from Burton's original glass negatives in the Metropolitan Museum's Photograph Studio, with the help of William F. Pons, Walter Yee, and Kenneth Campbell.

The black and white photographs of catalogue nos. 4, 16, 17, 19, and 24 were supplied by Helen Murray and Fiona Strachan of the Griffith Institute in Oxford; these are copyright by the Griffith Institute, Ashmolean Museum. Some photographs for catalogue nos. 3, 6, 7, 43, and 55 were made from Ektachromes by Lee Boltin.

Editors: Katharine Stoddert Gilbert, with Joan K. Holt and Sara Hudson
Design: Irwin Glusker, with Christian von Rosenvinge
Map and plan: Cal Sacks
Drawings for the catalogue entries: Patricia Johnson

Library of Congress Catalogue Card Number: 76–49920
ISBN 0-345-25684-0-795

Manufactured in the United States of America
First Edition: November 1976
Sixth Printing: June 1978

# FOREWORD

*Treasures of Tutankhamun* is the most important and beautiful exhibition of ancient Egyptian art ever to come to the United States. It differs in several key respects from the other presentations of selections from the remarkable contents of Tutankhamun's tomb held in this country in 1961-1963 and Japan in 1965, or in the landmark exhibition in Paris in 1967, organized by Mme. Christiane Desroches-Noblecourt, whose efforts paved the way for all subsequent Tutankhamun exhibitions, at the British Museum in 1972, and in the Soviet Union in 1974. The difference lies not only in the greater number of works of art—fifty-five in honor of the fifty-fifth anniversary of the discovery of the tomb by Howard Carter in November 1922—but in the basic theme of their overall presentation. Since almost fourteen hundred glass negatives made by the Metropolitan Museum's photographer Harry Burton throughout the course of the six-year excavation are at the Metropolitan, it was agreed by the participating institutions that these irreplaceable photographs and the actual objects would be brought together into a unique and complementary unity in the exhibition and the accompanying publications. An attempt has thus been made to suggest not only the excitement of the astonishing discovery of the tomb but, equally important, the painstaking and expert work entailed in the removal of the thousands of objects from the four jam-packed chambers of the relatively small tomb.

The works of art in this exhibition were chosen, accordingly, not only for their variety of subject matter, material, and sheer aesthetic beauty, but to give an accurate image of the contents of the four rooms of the tomb: the Antechamber, the Burial Chamber, the Treasury, and the Annex. In each of the six American museums, the fifty-five pieces are planned to be presented in approximately the same order, following as much as possible the manner in which they were originally excavated, as recorded in the Burton photographs and in Carter's list of objects.

The exhibition *Treasures of Tutankhamun* grew out of several years of discussions between a number of American museums and the Egyptian Organization of Antiquities. The final impetus for this long-hoped-for dream came during the visit to Egypt in June 1974 of President Richard M. Nixon, when President Mohamed Anwar el-Sadat expressed the hope that a splendid gathering of the masterpieces of Tutankhamun could one day come to the United States as a firm indication of the good will between the two nations. An accord toward this end was drafted and signed by Secretary of State Henry A. Kissinger and Foreign Minister Ismail Fahmy.

The precise details of the show and the schedule within the United States were then arranged between the professionals in the American museums and the Organization of Antiquities, under the guidance of the U.S. Department of State, represented by Peter Solmssen, Advisor on the Arts. At this time it was mutually decided that the Metropolitan Museum would act as the organizer of the exhibition. Subsequently it was agreed that income from the sale of printed materials and reproductions would be used, after expenses, for a project of fundamental importance to the cause of international culture. Everyone agreed that no project would be more fitting than the renovation of the Cairo Museum, a task to be undertaken over a number of years by the Organization of Antiquities with The Metropolitan Museum of

Art as consultant. Preliminary plans at present include the installation of a fire-control system in the Cairo Museum and the reinstallation of the Tutankhamun treasures in expanded quarters, using the same chronological and archaeological theme and equipment as the United States exhibition.

In the complex series of undertakings connected with this exhibition, hosts of individuals and their ideas have been brought together in the most perfect coordination possible. All who have contributed toward the existence of the exhibition deserve the utmost praise and thanks: Drs. Yussef es-Sebai and Gamal el-Outeifi, the Ministers of Culture and Information of Egypt under whose tenure the exhibition came to fruition; Dr. Mohamed Gamal ed-Din Mokhtar, President of the Organization of Antiquities, the guiding light of the exhibition; his chief assistant Dr. Ahmed Kadry and Council members Kamal el-Malakh and Dr. Rashid el-Nadouri, who guaranteed the smooth achievement of the show; Dr. Abdel Qader Selim, Director General of the Cairo Museum and his able curatorial staff, Dr. Dia Abu-Ghazi, Ibrahim el-Nawawy and his assistants Mme. Ghazabiyah Yahya and Hélène Nakla Michel, Mohammed Ahmed Mohsen, Dr. Ali Hassan, Salah ed-Din Ramadan, and Abdel Hadi el-Khafif; the conservation staff of the Cairo Museum headed by Dr. Salah Ahmed Salah, working with the Metropolitan conservators Christal Faltermeier and Rudolf Meyer; Dr. Fuad el-Oraby, Chief of Special Projects for the Organization of Antiquities; Dr. Christine Lilyquist, Curator of Egyptian Art of the Metropolitan, and members of her staff, Thomas Logan and Lynn Liebling; Dr. I. E. S. Edwards, whose expertise is evident in the entries prepared for the publications, and Dr. Edward F. Wente of the Oriental Institute in Chicago, for his contribution to the catalogue; Richard R. Morsches, the Metropolitan's Vice-Director for Operations; John Buchanan, Special Assistant to the Director of the Metropolitan; Irvine Mac Manus of the Metropolitan Museum, coordinator of the exhibition; William Harrison, President of International Business Associates, Cairo, and his assistant Georgia El-Monasterly, business representatives of the Metropolitan in Egypt; John Dorman of the American Research Center in Egypt; Christine Roussel and Bruce Hoheb of the Metropolitan's staff, who made the molds and models for the extensive series of reproductions that accompany the exhibition; Lee Boltin, the gifted photographer whose work graces this and other publications celebrating the exhibition; Bradford D. Kelleher, Publisher of the Metropolitan; Ian Pearson of the firm of Wingate and Johnson, who packed the objects and supervised their shipment; Mme. Christiane Desroches-Noblecourt, Curator of Egyptian Art at the Louvre, for her sage advice throughout the proceedings; and Stuart Silver, Director of Design of the Metropolitan and his colleagues. The National Gallery of Art in Washington deserves particular thanks for the design of the educational graphics, with the text written by William J. Williams of the National Gallery and Dr. David P. Silverman of the Oriental Institute of The University of Chicago. We are also grateful to Gaillard F. Ravenel of Washington, Larry Klein of Chicago, Franklin Adams of New Orleans, Jeanne d'Andrea of Los Angeles, and Neil Meitzler of Seattle in matters of design.

It should also be recorded that without the Arts and Artifacts Indemnity Act signed into law by President Gerald R. Ford on December 20, 1975, which provides full insurance coverage for these incomparable masterpieces, it would have been extremely difficult, if not impossible, to have mounted the exhibition. The indemnity for this exhibition was granted by the Federal Council on the Arts and the Humanities, and we are most appreciative of the patience and cooperation of the Council's able

*Overleaf: A scene during the complicated process of opening Tutankhamun's three coffins in the cramped confines of the Burial Chamber. The lower half of the outermost coffin is being lowered by ropes back into the stone sarcophagus; the second coffin is suspended on wires, and will eventually be placed on planks over the sarcophagus while it is opened. Howard Carter was puzzled by the coffins' immense weight; he was shortly to discover the reason — the third coffin was made of solid gold*

5

Executive Secretary, Lanni Lattin. In addition, it is important to pay tribute to the idea and efforts of the Honorable Herman Eilts, Ambassador of the United States to Egypt, to arrange through Admiral James L. Holloway III, U.S.N., Chief of Naval Operations, and Admiral David H. Bagley, U.S.N., Commander-in-Chief of the United States Naval Forces in Europe, for the use of two vessels of the Sixth Fleet, the U.S.S. *Milwaukee* and the U.S.S. *Sylvania*, which in the course of normal rotation to the United States – and consequently at no expense to the taxpayer – were able to transport the treasures of Tutankhamun to our shores with precise gentleness.

As it has done so many times in the past with exhibitions that have had a major impact in the areas of education and the humanities upon millions of Americans, the National Endowment for the Humanities, under the leadership of Dr. Ronald S. Berman and his assistant Nancy Englander, provided major financial assistance. In the case of the Tutankhamun exhibition, the NEH has matched generous grants from Exxon Corporation and the Robert Wood Johnson Jr. Charitable Trust. The continuing enlightened support on the part of Lila Acheson Wallace for the preservation and safekeeping of ancient Egyptian antiquities and her deep concern for the renovation of the Cairo Museum have been major factors in the presentation of this remarkable exhibition.

In conclusion, the directors of the participating institutions would like to thank the many members of our professional staffs, whose dedicated, creative, and cooperative labors brought *Treasures of Tutankhamun* to the six cities and the hundreds of thousands of visitors who will have the opportunity to see these extraordinarily beautiful works of art.

NATIONAL GALLERY OF ART
J. Carter Brown, *Director*

FIELD MUSEUM OF NATURAL HISTORY
E. Leland Webber, *Director*

ORIENTAL INSTITUTE OF THE UNIVERSITY OF CHICAGO
John A. Brinkman, *Director*

NEW ORLEANS MUSEUM OF ART
E. John Bullard, *Director*

LOS ANGELES COUNTY MUSEUM OF ART
Kenneth Donahue, *Director*

SEATTLE ART MUSEUM
Willis Woods, *Director*

THE METROPOLITAN MUSEUM OF ART
Thomas Hoving, *Director*

HONORARY COMMITTEE TO THE EXHIBITION
Ismail Fahmy, *Minister of Foreign Affairs of the Arab Republic of Egypt*
Gamal el-Outeifi, *Minister of Culture and Information*
Mohamed Ashraf Ghorbal, *Ambassador from the Arab Republic of Egypt to the United States*
Mohamed Gamal ed-Din Mokhtar, *President of the Egyptian Organization of Antiquities*
Ahmed Kadry, *Vice-President of the Egyptian Organization of Antiquities*

# THE DISCOVERY OF TUTANKHAMUN'S TOMB

TOM BUCKLEY, Reporter for *The New York Times*

On October 28, 1922, Howard Carter summoned his *reis*, the foreman of his excavating crew, to his house just outside the Valley of the Kings and told him that he wanted to resume work without delay.

Archaeologists worked only a short season in the Valley in those days. By April the pitiless sun, beating on its sheer rock walls, turned it into a furnace until late October, and the *khamsin*, the searing wind from the south, swirled its sandy floor into choking storms.

Carter had even less time than that. The tourists would begin arriving by mid-December to visit the burial ground of the pharaohs. Since his dig would block the entrance to the tomb of Ramesses VI, one of the Valley's most popular attractions, he knew he would have to be finished by then.

And this short season might well be Carter's last in the Valley. He had just returned from a meeting in England with the Earl of Carnarvon, who had been bearing the cost of his excavations for the past fifteen years and sharing in the infrequent glory of their finds. Carnarvon, disappointed by years of failure, told Carter that he had decided not to apply for the renewal of his government concession to excavate in the Valley. Only Carter's pleading, and his offer to pay the cost himself if nothing were found, had induced Carnarvon to agree to one final season.

So Carter knew that he had less than two months to complete, in success or failure, the search that had obsessed him for ten years. The prize he sought was the tomb of Tutankhamun, who had reigned more than 3,200 years before.

The Valley of the Kings, the royal necropolis, had been part of ancient Thebes, the capital from which the Egyptian empire was ruled at the zenith of its power. The Valley lay just a few miles away from the west bank of the Nile, whose unfailing waters nurtured Egyptian civilization, opposite Karnak and Luxor and more than four hundred miles south of present-day Cairo.

With the end of the seemingly perpetual power of the pharaohs, Thebes had been possessed by the Persians, by the Greeks of Alexander the Great, by the Romans, by the Arabs, by the Ottoman Empire. Egypt had been invaded by the French of Napoleon, who brought with him a group of scholars; later Egypt became a protectorate of Great Britain, although with its own ruling house.

For centuries the Valley and its surrounding desert, wild and inaccessible, had been the haunt of bandits. Only in the nineteenth century, as a measure of order was imposed, did archaeologists dare to begin excavating there.

In all, about thirty-three royal tombs had been found in the bedrock of the Valley or delved into its furrowed rock walls, but every one had been pillaged long before by professional thieves, some of whom struck within a few years of the royal burials. What had been found by Europeans, while it included many beautiful objects, was scarcely more than their leavings. At that, few important discoveries had been made in the Valley since the start of the twentieth century, and most experts believed that the burial ground had yielded all its secrets.

Carter, who had spent more than thirty years in Egypt, disagreed. Three

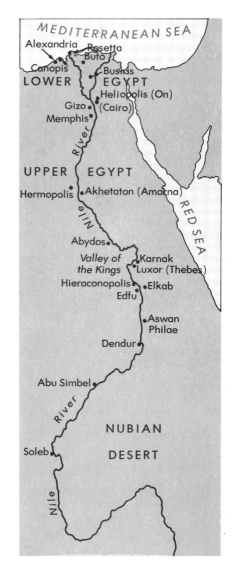

In a photograph taken around 1907, the man at the left is standing near the pit in which Theodore M. Davis found vessels containing materials used for mummifying Tutankhamun and the remains of his funerary banquet, a discovery that encouraged Howard Carter in his search for Tutankhamun's tomb. In the center of the picture can be seen the entrance to the tomb of Ramesses VI; the huts of the workmen who constructed it had been built over the opening to Tutankhamun's tomb, discovered about fifteen years after this photograph was made

discoveries made early in the century had reinforced his belief that Tutankhamun's tomb was hidden somewhere in the Valley. The first was a faience cup, found hidden under a rock, bearing the pharaoh's name. The next was a small, mud-filled pit tomb containing pieces of gold foil with pictures and inscriptions of Tutankhamun and his wife. The third was a cache of pottery jars—sealed with Tutankhamun's seal—that contained linen wrappings used in mummification, mourning wreaths, and other paraphernalia connected with ancient Egyptian funerary rites.

The finder, a rich, elderly American named Theodore M. Davis, who paid for the work of professional excavators, just as Carnarvon paid for Carter's, stated that he had found Tutankhamun's tomb. When the laughter of professionals at this absurd statement abated, the chastened Davis laid aside his discoveries as valueless.

But H. E. Winlock, director of the Metropolitan Museum's excavations at Thebes, visited Davis, examined the jars and their contents, and, with the permission of Davis and the Egyptian government, had them sent to the Metropolitan Museum where he could study them more carefully. Winlock realized that these funerary materials might imply the presence of a nearby tomb and, later, told Howard Carter about his conclusions.

In those days, to prevent the Valley from becoming a battlefield of rival archaeologists, the Egyptian government granted each year an exclusive concession to excavate there. When Davis, certain that nothing remained to be found, decided in 1914 to relinquish the concession, Carter persuaded Carnarvon to take it up.

By then, Carter had developed a theory as to where the tomb might be found.

His research indicated that only one small area of the Valley had not been cut across with archaeologists' trenches down to bedrock. This was a small triangle bounded by the tombs of Ramesses II, Merneptah, and Ramesses VI. One reason it had not been explored was that it was heaped high with rubble that had been excavated when the tomb of Ramesses VI, who lived about two hundred years after Tutankhamun, had been dug.

Tutankhamun, it appears, ascended the throne at the age of nine or thereabouts in about 1334 B.C., during the Eighteenth Dynasty. His parentage is uncertain, but it is known that he was married while still a child to Ankhesenamun, the third daughter of the famous Nafertiti.

The reign of Tutankhamun lasted only about nine years. It was a period of economic prosperity but of some religious confusion. Tutankhamun had been named Tutankhaton at birth, the last part of his name being a sign of his family's devotion to the Aton, the solar disk. During his reign the priestly orders of the kingdom, which still yielded greatest reverence to Amun, "the hidden one," were able to wield enough influence to have the young king change his religious allegiance. Tutankhamun died when he was eighteen or nineteen; the cause of his death is unknown.

Even assuming that Tutankhamun's tomb lay in the Valley – some experts thought it might have been buried outside of it because of the religious controversy – Carter faced a difficult task in looking for it even within the comparatively small area in which he had decided to concentrate his search. Just to reach the floor of the Valley, tens of thousands of tons of rock and sand would have to be removed by men filling rush baskets, and boys carrying them to vacant ground, emptying them, and returning – actions slowly and laboriously repeated millions of times.

It was a daunting project, and Carter had scarcely started to make his plans when the First World War began. Past the age of military service, Carter served as a King's Messenger, a diplomatic courier, in the Middle East. He visited the Valley when he could get leave, but it was not until the season of 1918/1919 that the work really began.

By the season of 1920/1921 Carter's workers had found the remains of huts used by laborers in the burial ground near the tomb of Ramesses VI. Thinking it unlikely that officials of the royal necropolis would have permitted such humble structures to be built atop a pharaoh's tomb, Carter spent the next season digging without success in another part of the Valley.

It was in the summer of 1922 that Carter returned to England to talk about the future of their dig with Carnarvon. By then the two men had been associated for fifteen years. Except for Egypt, they had little in common. Carnarvon, who was fifty-six, had attended Eton and Cambridge. He had traveled widely. He owned 36,000 acres of farmland. His ancestral seat, Highclere, in Berkshire, was one of the stateliest of the stately homes of England. He was a collector, a photographer, the owner of a large and successful racing stable. Although he was a votary of the cult of the thoroughbred, he was also an automobile enthusiast.

Indeed, it was Carnarvon's injuries in one of the first serious automobile accidents that led to his interest in Egyptology. While motoring through Germany in 1902 his car hit a farm wagon and overturned. Carnarvon was seriously hurt. The long, damp English winter became difficult for him. The next year he sought the warm, dry air of Luxor. Aside from agriculture in the narrow fertile strip along the Nile, tourists and archaeology were Luxor's only activities. Not wanting to reproach himself for wasting his time, Carnarvon decided to take up excavation. After a couple of years of false starts, he was introduced to Carter, and they hit it off from the beginning.

In 1922 Carter was forty-nine years old. He had grown up in provincial Norfolk, the son and grandson of animal painters, specialists who catered to Victorian England's love for its dogs and horses. He studied art at his father's knee but had little formal education.

In 1890 he first went to Egypt as a draughtsman with the Egypt Exploration Fund. He left the Fund to become an inspector in the Egyptian government's Department of Antiquities. After several years he was dismissed because of an incident involving a party of French tourists who were visiting the pyramids and tombs of Sakkara. The tourists became unruly and the tomb guards appealed to Carter; Carter, convinced that they were misbehaving, ordered them to leave. They protested, in vain, and then lodged a furious protest with their ambassador, whose guests they were. An apology was demanded of Carter by his superior. He refused and was fired.

Carter, intense, driven, a bachelor, must have received a nasty jolt that day at Highclere when the earl said he had decided to drop the concession. He had spent £20,000 – well over $500,000 in today's dollars – and all he had to show for it was holes in the sand.

One last season, Carter asked. If the tomb were not found, he said, he would pay for the work himself. Carnarvon relented, and Carter hurried back to Egypt to get started on his last clear shot at finding the tomb.

On November 1, two days after his conversation with his foreman, work was resumed. Fifty men and boys, happy to be employed from sunrise to sunset for wages of a shilling or less a day, began digging around the line of huts that Carter had abandoned a few seasons before. He had no choice; there was no place else to look.

In the next two days a layer of flint chips was uncovered. It was a mildly encouraging discovery, since rocks of this type were often used to block the entrance of royal tombs.

By the morning of November 4 the trench had been dug to bedrock, and to within fifteen feet of the entrance of the tomb of Ramesses VI. When Carter arrived from his house that morning, he found his workers just standing around.

"By the solemn silence all around caused by the stoppage of work, I guessed that something out of the usual had occurred," he wrote later. "My *reis* (foreman) was most cheerful, and confidentially told me that the beginning of a staircase had been discovered beneath the first hut removed."

Working slowly and carefully under Carter's eye, the workmen began clearing the staircase. The top of a doorway came into view. And on the plaster covering that sealed the door were affixed the seals of the royal necropolis – the jackal god Anubis above nine defeated foes.

"It was a thrilling moment for an excavator in that valley of unutterable silence, quite alone save for his native staff and workmen," Carter wrote, "suddenly to find himself, after so many years of toilsome work, on the verge of what looked like a magnificent discovery."

At that, Carter wrote, he did not dare to hope that he had actually found the tomb of Tutankhamun. The entrance seemed too modest; the setting was somehow wrong. But it might well have been a cache of royal objects or the tomb of a royal relative. What was important was that no one had known it was there and it still bore the seals on the door.

A more impetuous man might have continued to dig and satisfy his curiosity,

*The sixteen stairs leading down to the entrance corridor of Tutankhamun's tomb*

but Carter ordered the stairway filled again. He posted guards and hurried to Luxor to send a cable to Carnarvon. It read, "At last have made wonderful discovery in valley; a magnificent tomb with seals intact; re-covered same for your arrival; congratulations."

Carnarvon replied that he would arrive in Alexandria on November 20 with his daughter, Lady Evelyn Herbert. Nowadays the trip from London to Luxor can be made in five or six hours; then it took a week or more, by ferry across the English Channel, by train across France, by ship from Marseilles, and then by train from Alexandria to Luxor.

They were ferried across the Nile to the west bank and rode on donkeys through the narrow cultivated strip of fertile land, and then for five miles on the rough track into the desert to Carter's house, dark and cool, built of bricks of river mud, outside the entrance to the Valley of the Kings.

The next morning, their donkeys carried them to the site of the excavation. Carter and his assistant, A. R. Callender, had already begun clearing the stairway again. As more of the doorway was exposed, the seals of Tutankhamun could be seen in addition to those of the royal necropolis. When all sixteen steps had been cleared and the entire doorway could be seen, Carter got a jolt. Holes had been cut into the upper part of the door. The damage had been repaired and bore the seals of the necropolis, but the question remained: had this tomb, too, been pillaged?

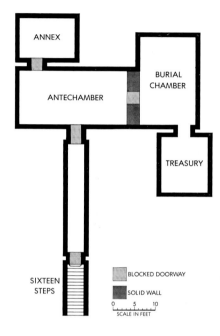

The door was removed, revealing a passageway cut through bedrock and filled with rubble. But here also there were indications that a tunnel had been cut through the filling, thousands of years before. Seated on folding chairs, shaded by parasols, Carnarvon and his daughter tried to contain their excitement while the passage was cleared. It ended in another sealed doorway twenty-five feet from the entrance, but it, too, had been cut through and repaired.

"The next day following," Carter wrote of November 26, "was the day of days, the most wonderful that I have ever lived through."

With Carnarvon, his daughter, and Callender standing behind him, Carter drilled a small hole in the upper left-hand corner of the door.

"Darkness and blank space, as far as an iron testing-rod could reach, showed that whatever lay beyond was empty," he wrote. "Widening the hole a little, I inserted the candle and peered in. . . . At first I could see nothing, the hot air escaping from the chamber causing the candle flame to flicker, but presently, as my eyes grew accustomed to the light, details of the room within emerged slowly from the mist, strange animals, statues, and gold—everywhere the glint of gold.

"For the moment—an eternity it must have seemed to the others standing by— I was struck dumb with amazement, and when Lord Carnarvon, unable to stand the suspense any longer, inquired anxiously, 'Can you see anything?' it was all I could do to get out the words, 'Yes, wonderful things. . . .' "

Aside from the fact that the objects that Carter was gazing upon, not to mention those that lay elsewhere in the tomb, were priceless, the Antechamber looked like the back room of a rummage shop. Parts of three ceremonial beds, thrones, countless vases, chariots, magnificently inlaid boxes, statuettes, weapons, and much else besides—the objects of luxury, comfort, and religious significance buried with the pharaoh for his voyage through eternity, and the greatest find in the annals of archaeology—lay in untidy heaps.

What had happened, Carter decided, was that the tomb had been ransacked not once but twice, probably within a comparatively short time after the burial.

The first time the robbers, possibly with the connivance of corrupt guardians, had carried away gold and semiprecious stones, since mountings and parts of missing objects were found. The second time they had apparently taken the costly oils and unguents from the tomb, pouring them from their heavy vases into less fragile skin bags.

Carter and his group went no further that day. Infinitely demanding work lay ahead if his find was to be handled with the care it deserved. Even so, he could scarcely have imagined that it would occupy him for the next ten years.

His workmen put two heavy wooden doors that he had already had made in place. They were locked and his foreman and the most trustworthy of his assistants remained on guard, while the four Britons departed.

"We mounted our donkeys and rode home down the valley," Carter wrote, "strangely silent and subdued."

The next morning Carter set up a portable electric lighting system. That afternoon he and Carnarvon, his daughter, and Callender removed the door and entered the chamber.

"Packed tightly . . . were scores of objects, any one of which would have filled us with excitement under ordinary circumstances," he wrote, "and been considered ample repayment for a full season's work. . . . Nor was it merely from a point of view of quantity that the find was so amazing. The period to which the tomb belongs is in many respects the most interesting in the whole history of Egyptian art, and we were prepared for beautiful things. What we were not prepared for was the astonishing vitality and animation which characterized certain of the objects."

Reports of the discovery had begun to circulate through Luxor, and Carnarvon decided that the time had come for an official announcement. It was made at a ceremony at the tomb on November 29, at which Lady Allenby, the wife of Britain's High Commissioner to Egypt, and a number of Egyptian notables were present.

In his days with the Egypt Exploration Fund, Carter had worked under the direction of Sir William Flinders Petrie, the father of scientific excavating technique, and he was determined that in dealing with his great find he would make Sir William proud of him. Since his own experience was entirely practical, he knew he would need academic and technical assistance, and he did not hesitate to seek it before starting to clear the tomb.

On December 3, therefore, he ordered the tomb closed and the passageway filled in. Then he and Carnarvon and Lady Evelyn Herbert – they were returning briefly to England – set off for Cairo.

On his arrival, Carter found a congratulatory cable awaiting him from A. M. Lythgoe, the curator of the Metropolitan Museum's Egyptian Department. In his reply, Carter asked if he might borrow the services of Harry Burton, the photographer with an excavating group sponsored by the Museum that was working just beyond the Valley.

"He promptly cabled back," Carter wrote, "and his cable ought to go on record as an example of disinterested scientific cooperation: 'Only too delighted to assist in any possible way. Please call on Burton and any other member of our staff.' "

Burton photographed each of the four chambers in the tomb in great detail before anything was touched, and then photographed the thousands of objects after their removal. His pictures – many reproduced in this book – are extraordinarily handsome, an achievement all the more remarkable considering the conditions under which he had to work and the limitations of cameras and other equipment at the time. Carter also availed himself of the services of other members of the Metropolitan Museum's expedition: Walter Hauser, an architectural assistant, Lindsley F. Hall, a draughtsman, and Arthur C. Mace, an associate curator who was supervising excavations elsewhere in Egypt. Mace, indeed, collaborated with Carter on the first volume of his three-volume account of the discovery. It is from that work that Carter's observations quoted in this article are taken.

While he was in Cairo Carter also arranged for Alfred Lucas, a chemist, to help in preserving fragile objects as they were removed, and for experts in art and hieroglyphs to assist in examining them. He also enlisted the cooperation of the Egyptian government's Department of Antiquities, which at that time was headed by a Frenchman.

He also bought many bales of cotton and miles of bandages, packing boxes, and lumber, for wrapping and packing his treasures, preservative chemicals such as paraffin, photographic supplies, and even an automobile. Fearful that the tomb might somehow be looted despite the presence of three separate sets of guards—such robberies were practiced as a hereditary occupation in the villages around the Valley—he ordered a heavy barred steel gate for the entrance and the strongest available locks and chains.

By Christmas the removal of the contents of the Antechamber to an empty tomb nearby that had been set up as a storage area and laboratory could be begun, but it wasn't just a matter of picking them up and taking them out. The task required seven weeks of careful work.

"So crowded were they that it was a matter of extreme difficulty to move one without running serious risk of damaging others," Carter wrote, "and in some cases they were so inextricably tangled that an elaborate system of props and supports had to be devised to hold one object or group of objects in place while others were being removed. At such times life was a nightmare. One was afraid to move lest one should kick against a prop and bring the whole thing crashing down."

With the Antechamber cleared, Carter was able to turn his attention to the two sealed chambers that led off it. Both had also been entered by robbers. Carter looked first into the room nearly opposite the entrance, which he termed the Annex. It was found to contain articles similar to those in the Antechamber. It was in the other, which opened off the right wall, that Carter and his associates decided they would find Tutankhamun's tomb, and that was where they went to work next.

On February 17, 1923, Carter was ready to open the Burial Chamber. In addition to the twenty experts and Egyptian government officials who crowded into the Antechamber, brightly lighted with portable electric lamps, hundreds more stood in the brilliant sunlight outside the tomb. Among them were scores of representatives of the press. Ever since the original discovery of the tomb, excitement had been building around the world. Already the objects of the Antechamber had influenced women's fashion and jewelry. Popular songs were being written about the discovery, jokes were being told in vaudeville houses and music halls.

The one sour note was the fact that Carnarvon had sold the exclusive rights to the story to *The Times* of London, which in turn syndicated it to other newspapers around the world. Carnarvon and Carter and their associates spoke only to *The Times*, and only *The Times* man was admitted to the tomb. Competing reporters, standing hour after hour in the sweltering sun, straining for crumbs of information, were understandably outraged, and as a result were delighted to cable whatever scraps of

*Howard Carter and Lord Carnarvon breaking down the wall that blocked the entrance to the Burial Chamber; one of the large gilded shrines surrounding the sarcophagus can be seen in the background*

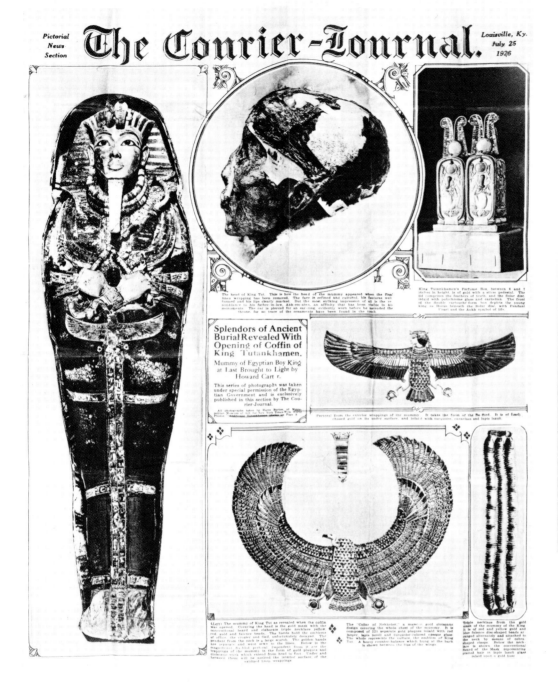

malicious gossip and rumor they could find. Carnarvon was puzzled by their attitude. The money was not the important thing: it was simply that Carter and his few co-workers, harried by the enormous job of excavating and recording thousands of objects, did not wish to have to keep answering the same questions a hundred times a day, or interrupting their work to lead parties of visitors through the cramped tomb with its fragile contents.

While the press gossiped in the sun, Carter chipped away at the stone and mortar with which the doorway to the Burial Chamber had been covered. "The temptation to stop and peer inside at every moment was irresistible," he wrote, "and, when, after about ten minutes' work, I had made a hole large enough to enable me to do so, I inserted an electric torch. An astonishing sight its light revealed, for there, within a yard of the entrance to the chamber, stood what to appearance

*Left: The lid of Tutankhamun's massive stone sarcophagus being raised, revealing the first of three coffins, shrouded in linen*

17

was a solid wall of gold."

The dazzled Carter quickly chipped away the rest of the filling. When he stepped inside he realized that what he was looking at was one side of a shrine that covered the sarcophagus of Tutankhamun. Made of wood covered with gold, it measured seventeen by eleven feet and was nine feet high, and filled the chamber except for a space about two feet wide between its sides and the rock walls.

In one wall was another doorway. It was unsealed. Looking within, Carter and Carnarvon, who had followed him into the Burial Chamber, saw still another astounding sight.

"Facing the doorway, on the farther side, stood the most beautiful monument that I have ever seen—so lovely that it made one gasp with wonder and admiration," he wrote. "The central portion of it consisted of a large shrine-shaped chest, completely overlaid with gold, and surmounted by a cornice of sacred cobras. Surrounding this, free-standing, were statues of the four tutelary goddesses of the dead—gracious figures with outstretched protective arms, so natural and lifelike in their pose, so pitiful and compassionate the expression upon their faces, that one felt it almost sacrilege to look at them." One of these exquisite statues, the goddess Selket, is illustrated in Color Plates 24-25.

It was not until the following season that the shrine and the three others inside it were entered, and the massive stone lid of the sarcophagus was lifted to reveal the pharaoh's coffin. Two others were nested inside it, the innermost one made of solid gold, beautifully chased and engraved, and about one-eighth of an inch thick. Within lay the linen-swathed body of Tutankhamun, gazed upon by mortal eyes for the first time in more than three thousand years. Covering his head and shoulders was one of the greatest of the world's artistic treasures—the polished gold funerary mask (Color Plate 12), elegant, calm, remote, and yet breathing with the life of a supremacy that had ended thousands of years before.

Carter gazed upon it, but Carnarvon did not. In April 1923, in Cairo, he had sickened and died. A mosquito bite had been nicked by his barber's razor; it had become infected, and then pneumonia had attacked Carnarvon's weakened lungs. His body was returned to England for a far simpler funeral than the pharaoh's. Trailing after it were whispers that caused goose pimples in the dark of night all over the world. From the day of the discovery of the tomb, gossip had whispered of the curse that fell upon anyone who violated a pharaoh's resting place. The press had picked it up, and now it seemed to come true. Who, after all, had ever died of a mosquito bite without yellow fever or malaria?

For years afterward, whenever anyone remotely associated with the discovery died, the story was revived. Travelers in the Middle East spoke jocularly of diarrhea as "King Tut's curse," just as in Mexico they call it "Montezuma's revenge." The biggest problem the curse theorists had was Carter. His fate should have been the most dreadful of all, but he lived on, full of honors, until 1939, when he died at the age of sixty-six, peacefully, at home in England.

Not for another year after the opening of the Burial Chamber were the intricate linen wrappings that swathed the mummified body removed. It was carefully examined by the leading pathologists of the time, but they were unable to establish the cause of the king's early death. In Tutankhamun's case the mummifying process was pretty much a failure. Too lavish use of precious oils and unguents, instead of preserving Tutankhamun's corporeal remains through eternity, had all but destroyed them.

# TUTANKHAMUN AND HIS WORLD

EDWARD F. WENTE, Professor of Egyptology,
Oriental Institute, The University of Chicago

Tutankhamun reigned from about 1334 to 1325 B.C., during the Eighteenth Dynasty of the New Kingdom, one of the most glorious periods of Egypt's long and distinguished history. About 3100 B.C. Egypt had become the first large state in history to be unified under a single king, when Lower Egypt (the area of the Delta) was conquered by the king of Upper Egypt (the Nile valley to the south of the Delta) and the "Two Lands" became one. During the next fourteen hundred years of Egyptian history, Egypt's inhabitants had enjoyed a measure of security from hostile powers, and in relative isolation had witnessed two major epochs, the Old Kingdom, noted for its pyramids, the Great Sphinx, and its confident art, and the Middle Kingdom, when the tone of the culture became more introspective.

The Sphinx and the pyramids of Giza were already ancient monuments by the end of the Middle Kingdom, around 1700 B.C., when political weakness permitted the peaceful infiltration of Asiatics into the rich Delta. Subsequently, while native pharaohs were usurping the throne in rapid succession, this Asiatic penetration became more violent, perhaps an invasion, and resulted in the burning and destruction of at least one important settlement in the eastern Delta. These Asiatics, known as the Hyksos, from the Egyptian expression meaning "rulers of foreign countries," eventually occupied the Egyptian capital at Memphis, near modern Cairo, and around 1665 B.C. they established themselves as the dominant political power in Egypt. The Hyksos overlords called themselves pharaohs, and, from their stronghold at Avaris in the eastern Delta, exacted tribute from the rest of Egypt.

The period of Hyksos domination, which was regarded by later Egyptians as a great humiliation, lasted about a century. Then a petty king in Upper Egypt who ruled at Thebes, more than four hundred miles south of the Hyksos capital, initiated a war of liberation. After a decade's lull in the fighting the foreigners were finally routed from their capital and expelled from Egyptian soil by the Theban king Ahmose. Because Ahmose had succeeded in unifying Egypt once again under native rule, he was regarded as the founder of the Eighteenth Dynasty, which lasted from 1570 to 1293 B.C.

The subjection and disarray of the Hyksos period was supplanted by new vigor and self-confidence. Egypt regained national pride as its armies scored victories in Asia and extended its frontiers in the south, effectively using two innovations it had picked up from the Hyksos, the horse-drawn battle chariot and the compound bow (examples of both were buried with Tutankhamun). The great pharaoh Thutmose III (1504-1450 B.C.) firmly established an Egyptian empire in Asia, after numerous campaigns in Palestine and Syria. In recognition of Egypt's dominance in this vital area of the Near East, other foreign powers such as Assyria, Babylonia, and the Hittites of Asia Minor sent gifts to the Egyptian king.

In creating this Asiatic empire Thutmose III did not resort to large-scale deportations of enemy populations, as some other Near Eastern powers did later in history, but a limited number of prisoners of war were taken back to Egypt. Some were donated to temples to serve in temple workshops, while others became household

*The mighty pharaoh Thutmose III smiting his enemies with a mace, on a wall in a temple at Karnak*

*Columns of the great Luxor temple built by Amenhotpe III and enlarged by Tutankhamun, whose work was usurped by his successor Haremhab. Across the Nile can be seen the Theban necropolis, with its temples and tombs. The Valley of the Kings lies behind the cliffs at the right-hand side of the picture*

slaves. And, in order to ensure the continued fealty of conquered city-states in western Asia, Thutmose III installed new princes and brought their sons or brothers back to Egypt to be educated. Some would eventually return to their homes to become loyal vassal princes, while others remained in Egypt to serve at the court. To quell insurrection and to supervise the regular delivery of tribute to Egypt, military garrisons were stationed at strategic points in Asia.

Thus Egypt, which previously had been relatively isolationistic in its political and cultural outlook, became involved in close contact with foreign cultures. Thutmose III — the Egyptian equivalent of Napoleon, a short-statured man curious about things foreign — even took an interest in Asiatic flora and fauna, bringing specimens home and donating them to the temple of the state god Amen-Ra at Thebes, the religious capital; they are carefully depicted in one of the halls of the great temple of Karnak at Thebes. Since in theory it was the god Amen-Ra who gave the king the power to achieve victories, much of the spoils of war and tribute was donated by the king to the temple or used to finance building programs on the god's behalf.

Not all foreign goods reaching Egypt at this time resulted from conquest.

During the Eighteenth Dynasty there existed commercial ties with other countries, both overland with Asia and Africa and by sea with lands of the eastern Mediterranean: Phoenicia, Crete, and the Aegean islands. The brightly painted tomb chapels of high officials contain scenes of processions of foreign delegates bringing goods that include Cretan wares, Syrian amphorae, and gold, ebony, ivory, hides, and exotic animals from Africa; evidence of such trade was found in Tutankhamun's tomb, such as two amphorae of Syrian type and several pieces of furniture featuring ebony and ivory. In this period the characteristic static quality of Egyptian two-dimensional art was often tempered through Minoan and Mycenaean influences that led to a freer treatment of the subject matter, especially in the rendition of movement. Some objects, such as the sheath of Tutankhamun's gold dagger (Color Plate 14), also reflect artistic influences of Near Eastern styles.

Eventually the cosmopolitanism that empire fostered even affected Egyptian religion. Under Amenhotpe II, Thutmose III's son and successor, we find evidence of the presence of foreign gods in Egypt: the important Canaanite deities Astarte and Resheph were revered in Egypt at first for their potency in warfare, but then became associated with similar Egyptian deities and were worshiped according to Egyptian cult practices. Conversely, the Theban god Amen-Ra came to be regarded as a universal god, concerned with lands beyond Egypt.

By the time of Tutankhamun's grandfather, Amenhotpe III (1386-1349 B.C.), Egypt was enjoying in full the fruits of empire, receiving rich tribute from the territories it controlled to the north and south. Warfare had subsided as international diplomacy increased. Peace with one of Egypt's most important foes, the kingdom of Mitanni in Syria, was ensured by the pharaoh's marriage to daughters of the Mitannian king. Foreigners believed gold was as plentiful as dust in Egypt, and Egypt's prosperity was reflected in the construction of huge temples, colossal statues of the pharaoh, and large and splendidly decorated rock-cut tomb chapels of high officials and courtiers in the Theban necropolis, located in the impressive desert hills on the west side of the Nile opposite the city of Thebes.

At the beginning of the Eighteenth Dynasty an attempt had been made to continue the practice of having a young pharaoh marry his sister, a marriage that had theological implications. Since the queen was regarded as the wife of Amun, the state god of Egypt, and the king was considered the god's son, a marriage between royal brother and sister stressed the divinity of the king. In the course of the dynasty this practice was modified; a number of kings who had been born of minor wives of kings were married to the most legitimate royal heiress to validate their own position in the succession. Amenhotpe III's much publicized marriage to Queen Teye, a commoner by birth, represented a significant break with the older tradition. Since her father Yuya was a commander of the chariotry one might see in their marriage an expression of the ever-increasing power of the military class, which earlier in the dynasty had provided tutors for young members of the royal family.

When Amenhotpe IV, the son of Amenhotpe III and Teye, acceded to the throne around 1350 B.C. (possibly as a co-regent with his father), he expressed devotion to the traditional gods of Egypt. But not long after the old king's death, Amenhotpe IV proceeded to institute a religious reform of sweeping nature: he selected one god, the sun god, to be the sole object of his veneration. Some scholars have interpreted this move as a political maneuver designed to terminate the growing power of the priesthood of Amun, which has been viewed as rivaling the throne even under Amenhotpe III. Although it is surmised, on somewhat erroneous grounds,

*Two daughters of Akhenaton and Nafertiti, depicted in a painting from Amarna (now in the Ashmolean Museum) with the informality and naturalism of the Amarna style. Their elongated skulls seem to have been a family trait: the portrait of Tutankhamun as a child in Color Plate 1 shows the same characteristic*

that Amenhotpe III had emphasized the solar cult at Thebes, there is no clear indication that this pharaoh experienced difficulties with the priesthood of Amun, of which his own brother-in-law was the second highest priest. Actually, Amenhotpe III's benefactions to the estate of Amun had been most extensive and were by no means confined to the sun god's cult, which was already present in a section of the temple of Amen-Ra that Thutmose III had erected at Karnak.

It would appear that Amenhotpe IV's motivation was less political than personal, and once having developed his iconoclastic religious ideas, he introduced them in a way that seems to reflect some planning. Without immediately terminating the cult of Amun, which lasted about four years into his reign, he first built a sanctuary at Karnak where the sun god Ra-Harakhty was identified with the Aton, the disk of the sun, but was still depicted in his traditional form, with the head of a falcon on a human body. The artistic style of this monument was conventional. By Amenhotpe IV's fifth year of rule, however, the anthropomorphic form of the sun god was for the most part eliminated, and the disk of the sun, with radiating rays ending in hands holding the symbols of life and dominion, served to represent Amenhotpe IV's view of a single, all-powerful god called the Aton, whose cult now entirely superseded Amun's at Thebes.

Just as radical as the theology was a new, naturalistic style of art that Amenhotpe IV fostered as expressive of the life-sustaining power of the Aton. In a sense this naturalism in art forms a parallel to the descriptions of nature in an idyllic hymn to the Aton that Akhenaton himself may have written. This hymn presents a fresh and lifelike description of universal exuberance over sunlight and life, realistically describing the joyous response of all living creatures to the life-giving powers of the sun, symbolized by the Aton. The hymn is singularly devoid of the clothing of myth so characteristic of earlier sun hymns as they expressed traditional religious beliefs, and may be considered as the culmination of Egyptian religious cosmopolitanism, since the Aton is described as concerned with all lands, providing for them "a Nile in the sky" — that is, rain, which was very rare in Egypt, whose inhabitants relied upon the Nile's annual flooding to cover their fields with fertile black silt.

It is thought that certain peculiar features of Amenhotpe IV's appearance—an elongated skull, protruding jaw, thick lips, slouching posture, and bulging stomach—were accentuated in the new art, and were carried over into representations of his queen, the beautiful Nafertiti, their children, and even commoners. The eccentricities of this new style were most pronounced during the early years of Amenhotpe IV's rule; later in his reign it became more polished and graceful. Traces of this style can still be seen in the decoration of certain objects from Tutankhamun's tomb, as, for instance, in the relaxed poses of the young king and queen on the exquisite throne back illustrated on page 24.

In accordance with his religious beliefs, Amenhotpe IV next altered his name from Amenhotpe, which means "Amun is content," to Akhenaton, which is probably to be translated "It goes well with Aton." On a virgin site at Amarna in Middle Egypt, about two hundred miles north of Thebes, he established a new capital called Akhetaton, meaning "Horizon of Aton." Here temples to the Aton were built: unlike traditional temples with their dimly-lit sanctuaries, these were entirely unroofed so the rays of the sun could penetrate everywhere and touch the king and queen wherever they proceeded in the temple, performing the daily services in honor of the Aton.

Throughout Egypt the temples of the old gods were shut down. The names and representations of the god Amun in particular were expunged from monuments, including temples and tomb chapels, and occasionally even the plural word "gods" was erased. Sacred images reposing in the shrines of the old temples were destroyed, while traditional rituals were abandoned and mythologies were discarded, being incompatible with Akhenaton's more rational religious thinking.

Although the new faith might appear to be monotheism, such an interpretation must be qualified by the fact that Akhenaton himself was considered to be divine, the son of the Aton and his living manifestation upon earth. The Egyptian pharaoh had always been thought to possess a divine quality, which, however, rested more in the office of kingship than in the king's person. Lacking the abstract concept of a state, Egyptians attributed the effectiveness of their collective endeavors to the pharaoh, in whose office the corporate personality of his subjects was represented.

But in the case of Akhenaton, the emphasis on his divine nature appears to have been intensified to the point that even his person was held to be divine. Unlike other kings, he, after the manner of a god, even had his own high priest during his lifetime. He may have sought to attain this unusual status by celebrating a jubilee festival very early in his reign, even before he moved the court to Amarna. One aspect of the jubilee ritual—usually celebrated in the thirtieth year of a pharaoh's rule—was the temporary identification of the king with the sun god, an apotheosis that served to reinvigorate the king. Inscriptions from Amarna, however, give the impression that Akhenaton's entire reign was a sort of perpetual celebration of the jubilee: one inscription proclaims, "The ruler is born like the Aton, enduring unto eternity like him in celebrating the million jubilees that the living Aton decreed for him." Since, according to the new theology, Akhenaton alone knew the Aton, everyone else essentially worshiped Akhenaton and only through his intermediacy the Aton. Thus the public apparently did not share in the ritual and worship of the Aton, which was performed by members of the royal family. In this respect the theology of the Amarna period afforded commoners considerably less direct access to the deity than did the older polytheistic religion with its cult images of the gods, which were periodically displayed in public to receive the adoration and petitions

*The back of a throne found in the tomb of Tutankhamun: it is covered with sheet gold, and the graceful figures of Tutankhamun and his queen are inlaid with colored glass and carnelian. Their clothes are made of silver. Above them shines the sun disk of the Aton, its rays ending in hands. Behind the queen is a table supporting a broad collar*

of people assembled in the temple forecourts. There was no sacred image of the Aton on earth save his bodily son Akhenaton.

A certain amount of iconographic and textual evidence indicates that Queen Nafertiti also partook of divinity in her relationship to her husband and the Aton, so that the three formed a sort of divine triad reminiscent of older groupings of three gods, such as Amún, the goddess Mut, and the child god Khonsu at Thebes. Viewed in this light, the depiction of the royal couple and their children in informal affectionate scenes, which occur often at Amarna, was probably less a diminution of their status than an illustration of a divine family.

Much has been written about Akhenaton's pacifism, supposedly inspired by the new theology, and the resultant decay of the Egyptian empire in Asia. At the time of Akhenaton the growth in power of the Hittite kingdom in Asia Minor was leading to a confrontation between Egypt and the Hittites, a development that also involved Syria and Phoenicia. An archive of diplomatic correspondence, written in the cuneiform script on clay tablets, was discovered at Amarna, and included among these letters between the Egyptian king and foreign rulers are frantic pleas of vassal princes asking for military aid, giving the impression that Akhenaton was uninterested in attending to what seems to be a disintegrating empire. However, there are indications that the Egyptian court was well aware that the rival Asiatic princes tended to portray the situation as worse than it actually was. Indeed, under Akhenaton military assistance was occasionally rendered to Asiatics if such action was deemed advisable in terms of the total picture of power politics. In addition, the fact that armed soldiers are frequently depicted in scenes from Amarna should serve to dispel the notion that Akhenaton was opposed to the use of the military on religious grounds. The decay of the Egyptian empire in Asia under Akhenaton seems to have been less extensive than formerly believed and was certainly not due to his disinterest or pacifism.

There is considerable controversy among scholars about the last several years of Akhenaton's seventeen-year reign. At some point in these final years, Smenkhkara – probably Akhenaton's son by a minor wife – was appointed co-regent and was married to Meritaton, the eldest daughter of Akhenaton and Nafertiti. By this time Nafertiti seems either to have died or to have withdrawn from the scene in retirement, although recently the novel theory has been proposed that Smenkhkara, one of whose names was identical with an epithet of Nafertiti, was none other than Nafertiti herself, who had adopted the trappings of kingship.

In Akhenaton's last year there seems to have been a resurgence of the cult of Amun at Thebes. There is some evidence that commoners had not totally relinquished their traditional beliefs, even in Akhenaton's capital: small amulets of the ancient deities Hathor and Bes were found in the workers' settlement at Amarna, suggesting that humble people had continued to cling to familiar household gods. The first suggestion of a return to orthodoxy outside Amarna occurs in an inscription from the third year of Smenkhkara's reign, perhaps while Akhenaton was still alive; it supplies evidence for a revival of the cult of Amun in a temple erected in the name of Smenkhkara at Thebes. One may suppose that at Thebes, where the persecution of Amun had been most intense, the ousted members of the Amun clergy and much of the local population harbored considerable resentment against Akhenaton's reforms. It has been speculated that Akhenaton may have sent Smenkhkara to Thebes to effect a reconciliation with the conservatives, but there is no positive evidence for any change of heart in Akhenaton himself, whose religious fervor seems to have intensified in the second half of his reign, when a great purge of Amun was carried out. Thus the renewal of the cult of Amun at Thebes may have been a response to local pressure rather than the result of an order from Amarna to reverse the tide.

Akhenaton seems to have died in 1334 B.C. and was probably buried in a tomb that had been prepared for him and Nafertiti in a desert valley to the east of Amarna. On the other hand Smenkhkara – whose death apparently occurred at about the same time as Akhenaton's – may have been interred in the traditional royal burial ground, the Valley of the Kings in western Thebes. A much disturbed and puzzling burial there contained the skeletal remains of a young man who may well have been Smenkhkara. Pathologists who have examined both these remains and Tutankhamun's mummy believe the two were probably full brothers. Certain funerary objects manufactured for Smenkhkara's burial were found in Tutankhamun's tomb: Smenkhkara's names were originally present – and were erased and replaced by Tutankhamun's – on both the miniature coffins containing Tutankhamun's embalmed viscera (Color Plates 26-27) and on some gold bands placed on his mummy. These objects, interestingly, do not reflect the theology of Amarna but traditional funerary beliefs associated with Osiris, god of the dead.

With the passing of Akhenaton and Smenkhkara, Tutankhaton – Tutankhamun's original name, meaning "Perfect is the life of Aton" or possibly "Living image of Aton" – came to the throne around 1334 B.C. as a boy of about nine years of age, a figure arrived at by subtracting the length of his reign of nearly ten years from the pathologists' estimate of his age at death. There is good evidence that Tutankhaton was the son of a king, and although there are inscriptions referring to Amenhotpe III as his father, chronological considerations now favor the view that he was actually Akhenaton's son, since the Egyptian word for "father" can also mean "grandfather" or "ancestor." Tutankhaton's mother may have been a minor wife of Akhenaton named Kiya, but was probably not Nafertiti, whose children, so far as we know, were limited to daughters.

During Tutankhaton's early childhood at Amarna, he was exposed only to the new religion and to the revolutionary naturalistic style of art. He was probably unaware of most of the traditions in religion and art: the images of the old gods, the ancient liturgies and myths were passé.

When he was still a child, Tutankhaton was married to Ankhesenpaaton, a daughter of Akhenaton and Nafertiti, and his legitimacy as king of Egypt was ensured. It is interesting to note that the two brothers, Smenkhkara and Tutankhaton, both married daughters of Akhenaton who seem to have been previously espoused to their own father, and possibly to have each borne a daughter by this incestuous marriage. Some scholars dispute these father-daughter marriages, but if Tutankhaton's age has been correctly ascertained by pathologists, he could not have fathered a child known as "Ankhesenpaaton Junior" during the first three years of his reign, the only time when he and his wife bore Atonist names.

Initially Tutankhaton and his court resided at Amarna, continuing the worship of the Aton, though perhaps with somewhat less fervor than when Akhenaton was alive. It was not long before traditional gods such as Amen-Ra and Mut infiltrated Amarna itself; there are a number of scarabs from the first years of Tutankhaton's rule at Amarna that mention Amun.

The appearance of elements of the traditional religion at Amarna at this time was perhaps spurred by the death of Akhenaton, who had been so closely identified with the Aton. The theology of Amarna had emphasized the Aton's continual revitalization of the living Akhenaton, but this philosophy failed to provide an adequate mythological answer to the problem of life after death, as did the older belief in Osiris, a god who had died and was then revivified to become the lord of the dead, and with whom the deceased identified. The Amarna theology made it impossible for the deceased king to be identified with Osiris, who was not officially recognized at Amarna. Perhaps unanswered questions regarding the fate of the dead Akhenaton led even those who had backed his cause to question the primacy of the Aton to the exclusion of the traditional gods.

During the first few years of Tutankhaton's rule at Amarna, it is possible that Nafertiti was still alive. The newly proposed theory that King Smenkhkara was in fact Nafertiti leads to further speculation that she was a regent for the young Tutankhaton; thus the restoration of the cult of Amun at Thebes, which was said to have occurred during Smenkhkara's third year of rule, might be assigned instead to the third year of Tutankhaton's reign, under Nafertiti's regency. This theory, however, leaves unanswered the question of the identity of the remains said to be Smenkhkara's.

Several of the objects buried with Tutankhamun probably date from his years at Amarna: these include pieces obviously designed for a child's use, such as a diminutive chair and a small bracelet (Color Plates 6, 17), as well as objects inscribed with the Atonist form of his name, such as a flail (Color Plate 5) and a scribal palette on which Tutankhaton is described as "beloved of Thoth, the lord of writing."

In the third year of Tutankhaton's reign, Amarna was abandoned as the capital in favor of Memphis and Thebes, and the Atonist names of the royal couple were altered from Tutankh*aton* and Ankhesenpa*aton* to Tutankh*amun* and Ankhesen*amun*, officially signifying their switch in devotion from the Aton to Amun.

During Tutankhamun's reign there was a tremendous amount of activity connected with the restoration of the old religion, especially at Thebes. The priesthoods, which had been dissolved by Akhenaton, were reconstituted, and new statues and images of the gods were made, some in the likeness of Tutankhamun himself. The majestic Luxor temple, which his grandfather Amenhotpe III had erected, was embellished with magnificent panoramas in painted relief, depicting in detail the great feast of Amun, which was revived in all its splendor. This festival involved a river procession of the elaborately decorated barges of the Theban gods, welcomed by crowds of jubilant Thebans. During the restoration Tutankhamun's ties with his grandfather were stressed, while the Amarna period was officially described as one during which the gods had withdrawn so that prayers were left unheeded. It is significant, however, that at this time there was no outright attack upon the Aton, who still remained a god, but no longer the sole one.

A number of pieces from Tutankhamun's tomb reflect the moderate attitude toward Atonism. In the charming scene portraying the king and queen in the Amarna style, illustrated earlier on page 24, the Aton disk is prominently featured while the king's name appears in its Amun form. However, on one side of this golden throne the Atonist name Tutankhaton appears. On another throne, inlaid in ebony and ivory, the sun disk is again prominent, and inscriptions contain the king's names in both forms. Among the king's epithets on this throne are references to Tutankhamun's close relationship to the traditional gods: he is called "the image of Ra, beloved of the gods" and "the son of Amun, whom he desired to be king." Conversely, an inscription on a tall-legged cabinet indicates that even after the restoration of the old temples, Tutankhamun could still be called "the eldest son of Aton in heaven."

Just as there is no evidence of an attack on the Aton under Tutankhamun, so there is no positive indication of the persecution of Akhenaton's memory during Tutankhamun's reign. Tutankhamun's tomb contained a box bearing the cartouches of Akhenaton and Smenkhkara, an artist's palette that belonged to Akhenaton's eldest daughter Meritaton, and the lid of a small box depicting Akhenaton's daughter Neferneferura. An estate of the Aton was still supplying the royal household with wine as late as the ninth year of Tutankhamun's reign.

The nature of the evidence pertaining to the return to orthodoxy under Tutankhamun suggests that a symbiosis of Atonism and Amunism existed for some time during his reign, and that the Amarna style of art continued. The golden shrine illustrated in Color Plates 8-9 bears a number of references to the traditional gods, but the scenes depicting the king and his queen are rendered in the freer style of art characteristic of the Amarna period.

Whereas Akhenaton's reformation had been intolerant of the existence of the old gods, the counter-reformation under Tutankhamun was more charitable and broad-minded. At issue was not the specific name of the god but the nature of the divine. A trumpet from Tutankhamun's tomb (Cat. no. 3) bears a scene of the king in the presence of the three major gods of the New Kingdom: Amen-Ra, Ra-Harakhty, and Ptah. A somewhat later hymn describes the relationship of these gods: "Three are all gods: Amun, Ra, and Ptah, and they have no counterpart. 'Hidden' is his name

*The photograph above was taken during the unwrapping of Tutankhamun's mummy: amulets and other funerary equipment made of gold can be seen, with the iron-bladed dagger at the left*

as Amun, he is Ra in the sight [of men], and his body is Ptah." The old theology of Egypt respected the divine as being both beyond human comprehension and yet manifest in the cosmos and in sacred images. Because the divine also acted in human terms, the Egyptian could even speak of recognizing "the god who is in man," believing that the deity does inspire man directly in guiding his heart. Under Akhenaton, it would have been more difficult to discern the divine in one's fellow man, for the emphasis at Amarna was that knowledge of the Aton was Akhenaton's prerogative, and he in turn "taught" his subjects. An account of Tutankhamun's reforms, known as the restoration stele, is quite explicit about the disruption of the relationship between god and man that had occurred as a result of Akhenaton's innovation that made the king an intermediary in man's approach to god. With the counter-reformation under Tutankhamun it was once again possible for men to encounter the gods directly.

Because of Tutankhamun's youth and Atonistic background, his active role in the return to orthodoxy must have been minimal. In fact, Tutankhamun possesses no personality about which the historian can talk. The achievements of his reign were probably less a result of his will than the activity of two important individuals: the vizier Ay and the general Haremhab. The aged Ay had had a close association with Amarna, where he served as overseer of all the king's horses, and where he had prepared an imposing tomb for himself; because of his attachment to the Amarna royal family, indicated by his title "God's Father," Ay was probably responsible for the moderation that characterized the return to polytheism. The similarity between Ay's titles and those of Yuya, Queen Teye's father, as well as connections both men had with the Upper Egyptian town of Akhmim, does lend some support to the theory that Ay was Nafertiti's father.

On the other hand, Haremhab, who must have been an army commander under Akhenaton, had less discernible associations with Amarna, nor did he have any blood relationship with the royal family. Born in Middle Egypt, Haremhab distinguished himself both as a general and as king's deputy under Tutankhamun. In Asia Haremhab seems to have achieved some success in reasserting Egyptian authority, which was being challenged by the Hittites. Any decline in Egypt's Asiatic relationships at this time may have been due less to any lack of military preparedness on Egypt's part than to the growth of Hittite power and influence in Asia. The text on Tutankhamun's restoration stele suggests Egyptian forces did function effectively in Asia under Tutankhamun, who elsewhere is said to have filled the temple workshops with male and female slaves captured abroad. Indeed, in Haremhab's tomb in Memphis, decorated under Tutankhamun, there are reliefs and texts suggesting that a delegation of Asiatic princes came to Egypt imploring aid against their enemies' incursions, while another scene from the same tomb depicts Asiatic prisoners.

The pharaoh is customarily shown singlehandedly defeating foreign enemies in royal reliefs of the New Kingdom, and on several objects from his tomb Tutankhamun is depicted vanquishing Egypt's foes. But this sort of evidence cannot be used as proof that Tutankhamun actually took part in military campaigns. The nature of the concept of the pharaoh was such that it was he who prevailed over enemies even in battles he had not personally fought. It is conceivable, however, that as Tutankhamun matured, he might have engaged in warfare: the pharaoh Amenhotpe II had campaigned in Asia at the age of eighteen. Thus it is remotely possible that Tutankhamun may have used in battle some of the bows that were discovered buried with him (Color Plate 28). Certainly he was trained in archery, for an inscription on the handle of a magnificent gold fan (Color Plate 11) informs us that its plumes, now disintegrated, were obtained from ostriches hunted by Tutankhamun on the desert east of Heliopolis, near modern Cairo.

As king's deputy Haremhab was also much involved in internal reconstruction and, perhaps more than Ay, was the dynamic power behind the throne. To the south Egypt was firmly in control of the Nubian gold mines, and in the Theban tomb chapel of Tutankhamun's viceroy of Kush are illustrated the products of Africa that contributed to making this an opulent age, which, thanks to the treasures contained in Tutankhamun's tomb, we are now in a position to appreciate. While we are apt to be most impressed by the amount of gold found in this tomb, several objects made of iron, including a miniature headrest and a beautiful dagger (shown on page 28), are of archaeological importance. Before Tutankhamun's time, iron objects are of extreme rarity, for Egypt was the last of the countries of the Near East to become an Iron Age culture. The smelting of iron on a significant scale seems to have been first achieved by the Hittites.

While the restoration of the old cults was still in progress, Tutankhamun suddenly died. Mystery surrounds his death. It has been observed that his skull exhibits some damage, which might be interpreted as indicating that he was assassinated, although it is possible that this injury occurred after his death. Also baffling are two mummified stillborn children, probably male and female, placed in his tomb. While they could easily be the dashed hopes of the royal couple for continuing their line, it has also been proposed that the fetuses were interred with Tutankhamun for religious reasons, to aid symbolically in the revivification of the

*A corner of the Treasury, the third chamber in Tutankhamun's tomb, its contents hastily tidied by the necropolis guards after an ancient robbery. A chest containing the mummified bodies of two stillborn babies, perhaps Tutankhamun's children, lies against the back wall*

dead king through the male and female principle.

Tutankhamun's early death seems to have caught him unprepared. Often, in the New Kingdom, the first year of a king's reign was characterized by the initiation of new projects, one being the construction of the king's future tomb in the Valley of the Kings. This was not the case, however, with Tutankhamun, who had come to the throne at Amarna. From the very modest size and arrangement of the chambers in which he was buried, it is obvious that his sepulcher was a hastily-converted commoner's tomb, not intended for a royal burial. The meagerly and not too expertly decorated Burial Chamber cannot compare either in quality or in extent of decoration with many of the royal tombs previously known.

Rather, Tutankhamun's tomb is famous for what it contained. Some objects were belongings that he had used during his life and might be expected to enjoy in the afterlife; some were strictly of a funerary nature, such as amulets to protect him during his travels through the underworld, and funerary statuettes with his visage and tools to perform any labors the gods might assign to him. The artisans had ten weeks to complete all the funerary equipment — the coffins, the shrines that protected them, and other requirements of the burial ceremony — since the process of mummification took seventy days.

The corpse was mummified on the west side of the Nile. After the internal organs, except the heart, had been removed, the body was packed in a dry mineral called natron for dehydration. Then resins, gums, and oils were used to embalm the body, which was carefully wrapped in linen bandages and adorned with amulets and other jewelry. Meanwhile, the liver, lungs, stomach, and intestines, which had been treated separately, were usually placed in four containers called Canopic jars. In the case of Tutankhamun, the organs were placed in four miniature coffins (Color Plates 26-27), which in turn were deposited in a Canopic chest, the four cavities of which were capped with lids bearing the king's likeness (Color Plate 12). The chest was enclosed in a shrine guarded by four statuettes of the goddesses Isis, Nephthys, Selket (Color Plates 24-25), and Neith.

After the mummy had been wrapped and provided with a mask, it was drawn on a canopied sledge to the tomb. Tutankhamun's sledge was hauled by the highest officials of the state, perhaps first to the funerary temple and then on to the tomb, where the interment of the pharaoh marked his entrance into the netherworld.

The aged Ay, who succeeded Tutankhamun as king, officiated at the young king's funeral and also completed a temple at Karnak that Tutankhamun had started. Perhaps it was Ay who encouraged Tutankhamun's widow to write a strange letter to the very man who was threatening the northern reaches of the Egyptian empire: she asked the king of the Hittites, Shuppiluliumash, to send her a Hittite prince for a husband, who could become king of Egypt since it would be improper for her to wed an Egyptian commoner. The Hittite king, suspicious of this appeal, sought further clarification from Egypt, and when he was convinced of the genuineness of the widow's plea, sent his son Zannanzash on his way to Egypt. Ay was old, and this extraordinary maneuver was perhaps the only hope the glorious Eighteenth Dynasty line had of perpetuating itself. But the Hittite prince was murdered before he reached Egypt; presumably Haremhab, as a nationalist, perceived the dangers inherent in this scheme and had the Hittite prince assassinated. The murder of Zannanzash did result in more vigorous Hittite military action against Egyptian outposts in Syria. The Asiatic wars of the Nineteenth Dynasty pharaohs Sethy I and Ramesses II never successfully recovered areas lost to the Hittites, who proved

*Part of the painted decoration in the Burial Chamber, this frieze depicts, from right to left: Tutankhamun's successor Ay, with the leopard-skin mantle of a setem priest, performing the important ceremony called "Opening the Mouth" on Tutankhamun's mummy, garbed as Osiris; Tutankhamun standing before the sky goddess Nut; and Osiris, god of the dead, welcoming Tutankhamun, who is followed by his spirit double*

to be a formidable foe until Ramesses II finally concluded a treaty with them and subsequently married Hittite princesses. Thus further indecisive wars in Asia were the price Egypt had to pay for maintaining a native Egyptian on the throne, but at least Egypt was spared the possibility of another foreign humiliation.

As a powerful general Haremhab had only to wait until Ay's death before he easily took over the throne. As pharaoh he sought to indicate more clearly the leading role he had played in effecting the restoration of the traditional gods and tried to obliterate the memory of his immediate predecessors by razing their monuments or by replacing the names of Tutankhamun and Ay with his own. As a result of this thorough pogrom, Egyptians of succeeding generations were little aware of the importance of the young king's brief reign.

But from what we have learned since the discovery of Tutankhamun's tomb, we can begin to piece together the story of the Eighteenth Dynasty. From rather humble beginnings this dynasty marked the conversion of Egypt from a land dominated by Asiatic overlords to a world power that controlled an important area of western Asia. Egyptian culture was vitally affected by the creation of empire, but ultimately a theological crisis developed that struck at the very roots of Egyptian religious thought. As a boy, Tutankhamun had grown up at a time when most Egyptians must have been confused by the new theology and art that Akhenaton promulgated. It was in Tutankhamun's short reign that the validity of traditions which had been challenged was reaffirmed in a spirit of reconciliation. There is some reason to suspect that the richness of Tutankhamun's burial was extraordinary, and some of the objects, like an elegant figure of the king's mummy (Color Plate 23), were actually donated by private citizens. Perhaps Tutankhamun's magnificent burial, with all its gilt and gold, was less a tribute to his youthful person than an expression of the community's feeling of relief at the restoration of the old gods and traditions. Perhaps Tutankhamun was, even in death, more of a concept than a personality.

# COLOR PLATES

**PLATE 1** As a work of art the painted
wooden figure shown at the right stands out
among the whole contents of Tutankhamun's tomb. It illustrates one of the most
picturesque ancient Egyptian accounts of
the initial creation: it represents the
infant sun god at the moment of birth,
emerging from a blue lotus that grew in a
pool left by the receding waters of the
primordial ocean. The features are unmistakably those of Tutankhamun, and the
shape of the elongated skull is very
reminiscent of the Amarna princesses who
may have been his half-sisters. By having
this model in his tomb, Tutankhamun,
through the process of imitative magic,
would have an instrument that would enable
him to be reborn as the sun god every
day. (Cat. no. 1)

The god of eternity, who is also depicted on
the handles of the wishing cup, dominates
the superbly carved panel on the back of
this ceremonial chair. Every detail has been
executed with the utmost feeling and
delicacy; the figure of the god possesses
elegance and grace, and each hieroglyph is
a work of art in itself. (Cat. no. 12)

**PLATE 3** Leopard-skin mantles were worn by many categories of Egyptian priests, and two – one a real skin, the other a cloth imitation – were buried with Tutankhamun for his use in the afterlife. This head, of wood overlaid with gold, belonged to the real leopard skin. (Cat. no. 4)

The stool above, with an inflexible seat firmly joined to the legs, imitates a folding stool with a leopard-skin seat. (Cat. no. 11)

**PLATE 4 (OVERLEAF)** Reversing the natural colors, the spots on the stool's leopard-skin seat are made of ivory, set in an ebony background. Leopards were extinct in Egypt in the New Kingdom, but their skins were regularly included among tribute sent annually from Nubia (Cat. no. 11)

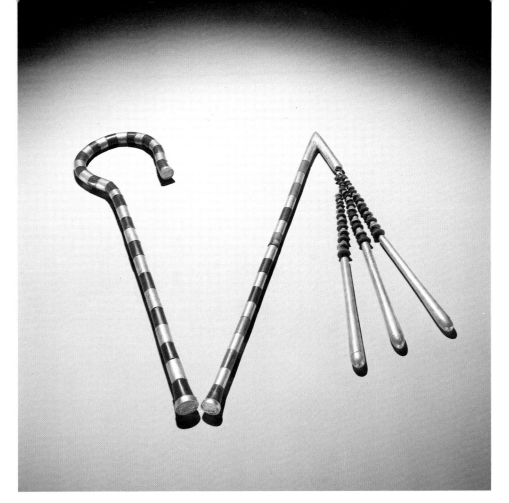

**PLATE 5** Some fifty alabaster vases, such as the one at the left, were found in the tomb, nearly all emptied of their precious contents by ancient robbers. (Cat. no. 10)

The crook and the flail were the insignia of the beneficent god Osiris, and were carried on some ceremonial occasions by the pharaoh. The flail shown here is inscribed with Tutankhamun's name in its original form, Tutankhaton, and it is possible that he carried it at his coronation when he was about nine years old. (Cat. no. 5)

Tutankhamun is represented on the golden buckle at lower right as a warrior returning from battle, his hound running beside his chariot. Taken as a whole, the design means that Tutankhamun, protected by the goddesses of Upper and Lower Egypt and supported by its inhabitants, will vanquish all his enemies. (Cat. no. 6)

**PLATE 6** Both in form and in construction, this chair is typical of its period. The wood, probably ebony, is decorated with ivory inlay and with gilded panels depicting ibexes and desert plants. Because of its small size – it is only twenty-eight inches high – it is thought to have been made for Tutankhamun when he was a child. (Cat. no. 8)

**PLATE 7**  The chests shown here are examples of the Egyptian craftsman's exquisite use of materials. The one at the left is made of ebony and a red wood, perhaps red cedar; it is the only known example of an ancient Egyptian portable chest. The casket below is carved of alabaster, with painted decoration. It bears the name of both Tutankhamun and his queen, and contained two balls of hair wrapped in linen, which are thought to indicate some kind of contract. (Cat. nos. 7, 9)

PLATE 8 The trumpet at the far left, made of bronze or copper with gold overlay, is one of three ancient Egyptian examples of this instrument; to the right is its wooden stopper, used with a cloth to clean it or to prevent its being damaged when not in use. Trumpets are perhaps the only ancient instrument whose exact sound can be reproduced today. (Cat. no. 3)

The small golden shrine at the right is in the form of the sanctuary of the vulture goddess Nekhbet. Every exposed surface is covered with scenes, inscriptions, or some other kind of decoration, all in relief. (Cat. no. 13)

**PLATE 9** The picture at left shows the interior of the golden
shrine (Cat. no. 13), with a pedestal that probably once
supported a golden statuette of Tutankhamun, stolen by the
ancient robbers. The imprint of the statuette's tiny feet can still be
seen. The scene above shows the king and queen in the relaxed
and informal poses that are a vestige of the Amarna style.
The king is seated on a stool that suggests the one in Color Plate 3.

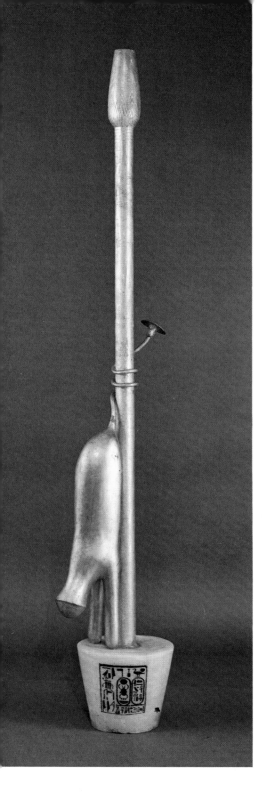

**PLATE 10** The eerie emblem at the left, made of gilded wood, is associated with the god Anubis: it depicts a headless animal skin attached to a pole, in an alabaster base. It harks back to very remote times, when real animal skins were swathed in bandages like a mummy and placed in tomb shrines. (Cat. no. 15)

The oil-burning lamp below, carved from a single piece of alabaster, represents a lotus plant growing from the bed of a pond. Slight traces of oil were still visible in the three cups when the lamp was first discovered. (Cat. no. 14)

The charming beast shown at the right may have been intended to suggest the king's lion-like character. Lively scenes of animals in combat are incised on the unguent jar beneath. (Cat. no. 16)

PLATE 11 Tutankhamun himself is shown hunting the ostriches whose feathers — now disintegrated — were used for the plumes of this fan. On the reverse (below), the dead ostriches are borne off by His Majesty's attendants. (Cat. no. 18)

The handsome gold case at the right was made to contain some kind of unguent. Both figures represent Tutankhamun, once with fair skin and, at left, with a black face. Although the color has no ethnic significance, its precise meaning is not easy to explain: it may symbolize regeneration. (Cat. no. 19)

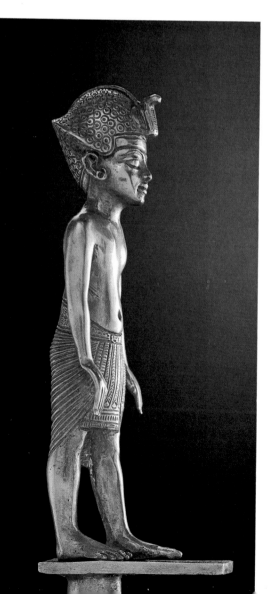

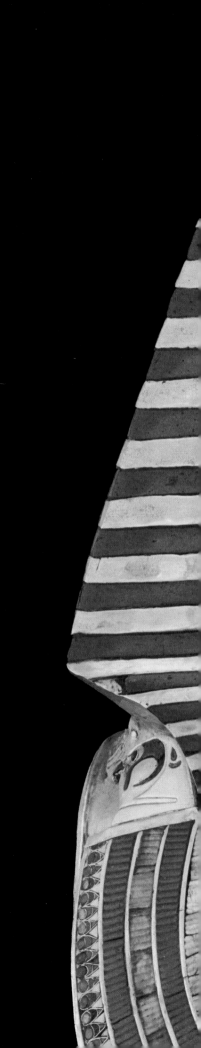

**PLATE 12** These are three portraits of Tutankhamun, as a chubby child (left) and then at the time of his death, about ten years later. The figure below is made of gold, and topped a staff that the young king may have carried at his coronation. (Cat. no. 17)

The portrait above is one of the four alabaster stoppers in a magnificent Canopic chest in which the king's internal organs were placed. (Cat. no. 44)

The mask at the right is probably the most famous work of art from Tutankhamun's tomb. Made of solid gold, it seems to be a faithful depiction of the king: the rather narrow eyes, fleshy lips, and shape of the nose and chin all agree with the features visible on his mummy. (Cat. no. 25)

**PLATE 13 (OVERLEAF)** This superb gold collar, inlaid with colored glass, was placed on the chest of Tutankhamun's mummy. In the form of the vulture goddess Nekhbet, it was intended to provide magical protection. (Cat. no. 23)

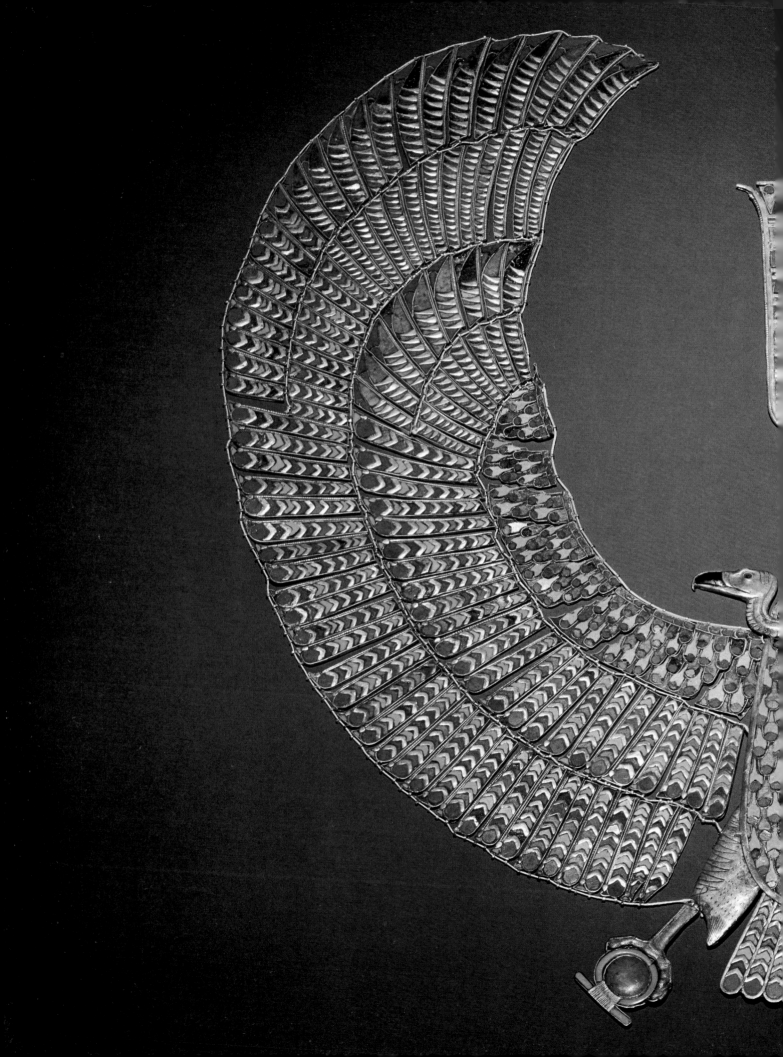

PLATE 14 Gold daggers were probably reserved for royalty, and this one is an outstanding illustration of the goldsmith's technical skill. Its simple blade is set off not only by the ornate haft but also by the richly decorated sheath, which includes artistic features with a foreign appearance. (Cat. no. 20)

This solid gold necklace, encrusted on the front with blue and red glass, was probably worn by Tutankhamun during his lifetime. The vulture goddess Nekhbet is shown holding the hieroglyphic sign for "infinity." On the reverse, Nekhbet is depicted wearing a necklace decorated with Tutankhamun's name. (Cat. no. 24)

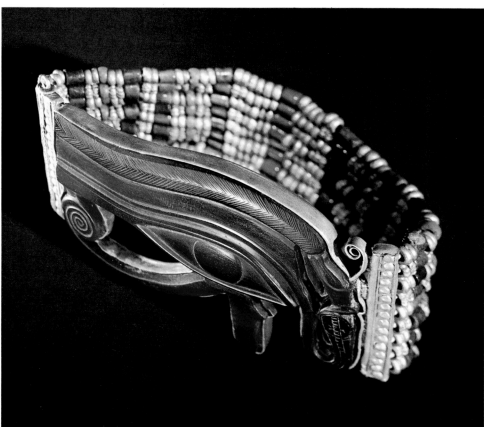

**PLATE 15** The bracelet illustrated in three views at the left was placed on the right arm of Tutankhamun's mummy. It depicts an *udjat* eye — a human eye and eyebrow to which are added the markings on a falcon's head. With the exception of the scarab, the *udjat* eye was the most popular amulet in ancient Egypt. It symbolized filial piety and was thought to be a potent amulet against sickness as well as capable of restoring the dead to life. (Cat. no. 21)

The heavy gold rings at the right depict some of the most important Egyptian deities, whose cults Tutankhamun restored after their suppression by his predecessor Akhenaton. (Cat. no. 22)

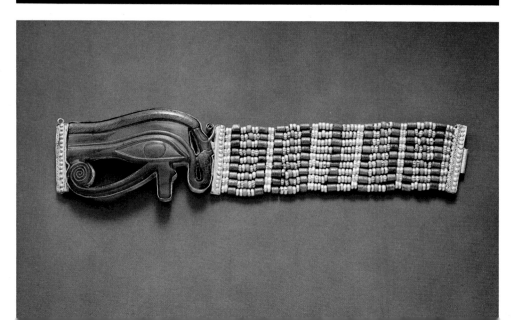

PLATE 16 This tiny figure of solid gold was found, wrapped in a piece of linen, within a gilded miniature coffin. It has been identified as Amenhotpe III, but it seems more probable that it represents Tutankhamun himself. (Cat. no. 41)

The elaborate pectoral at the left dramatically illustrates a fusion of two related symbols that were originally independent. In Egyptian art the sun god could be represented both as a scarab and as a falcon: here he is symbolized by a chalcedony scarab that serves as the body of a falcon with outstretched wings. It has the forelegs of a scarab and, at the back, falcon's legs. (Cat. no. 26)

The jewel at the right depicts the sun god as a falcon, a very ancient conception probably inspired by the falcon's habit of flying high in the air. In each talon it holds the signs for "life" and "infinity." (Cat. no. 27)

PLATE 17 The box at the left contained these earrings and the scarab bracelet shown below. Earrings, at least for royalty, were a relatively recent innovation at the time of Tutankhamun. They seem to have been worn by boys, who discarded them on reaching manhood. (Cat. no. 29)

This box is in the shape of a cartouche, the oval ring in which royal names were written. A cartouche actually represents a length of rope formed into a loop by tying the ends together, the underlying idea being to represent the king as ruler of all that the sun encircled. Here, the hieroglyphs at the top render Tutankhamun's personal name and his usual epithet. (Cat. no. 28)

The ancient Egyptians adopted the scarab as a symbol of the sun god because they were familiar with the sight of the beetle rolling a ball of dung on the ground, and this action suggested the invisible power that rolled the sun daily across the sky. The scarab on this bracelet, photographed under a mirror, is made of gold openwork encrusted with lapis lazuli. (Cat. no. 32)

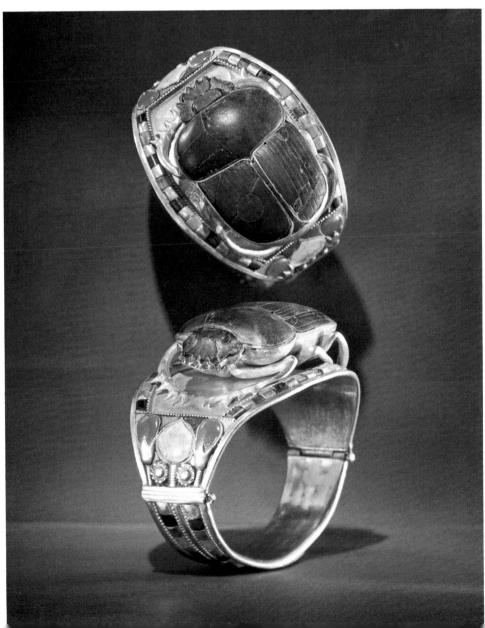

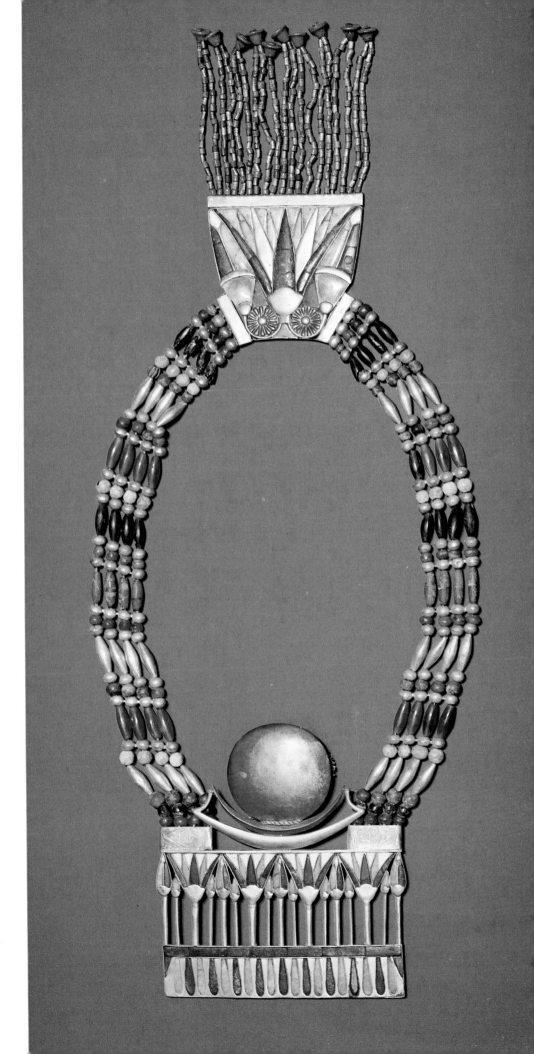

**PLATE 18** In the Egyptian language, a word for hand mirror was *ankh*, spelt like the word meaning "life." The artist who designed this mirror case in the form of the hieroglyphic sign for "life" was no doubt deliberately indulging in a play on words. (Cat. no. 30)

The pectoral on this lovely necklace symbolizes the nocturnal journey of the moon across the sky. A golden bark containing the moon (represented by a disk with crescent) floats above the sky sign in celestial waters from which lotus flowers grow. (Cat. no. 31)

**PLATE 19 (OVERLEAF)** On the next pages are shown details of this necklace: the gold counterpoise decorated with lotus and poppies, and the pectoral with the moon bark. The moon disk and crescent are made of electrum, a natural alloy of gold and silver, and the other parts of the necklace consist of gold, feldspar, lapis lazuli, carnelian, and dark-colored resin. (Cat. no. 31)

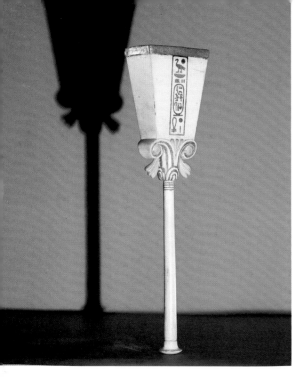

From the earliest times onward, the regular vehicle of transport in Egypt was the boat. Nature had provided a river that was navigable at all seasons, and sailing against the current was greatly simplified because the prevailing wind blew in

PLATE 20 A small group of articles used in writing was found in Tutankhamun's tomb, although he himself may not have been able to write. Among them were a handsome papyrus burnisher (Cat. no. 34) and a very elaborate pen holder (Cat. no. 33).

that direction. This model boat is one of seven of its kind that were stacked higgledy-piggledy in the Treasury of Tutankhamun's tomb. Since it has neither oars nor sail, it must represent a barge towed on some formal occasion. (Cat. no. 36)

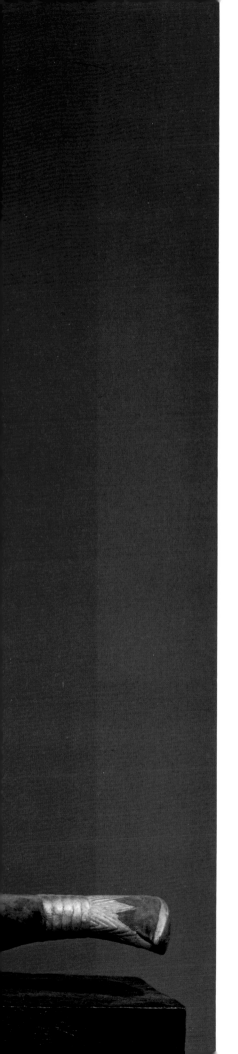

PLATE 21 This depiction of the pharaoh on the back of a leopard seems to have been connected with incidents in the passage of the king through the underworld. The leopard is black, the color of darkness, but it would have been inappropriate to depict the king in black because he was associated with the sun god, who brought a brief spell of light to the underworld as he passed through it each night. (Cat. no. 38)

The superb piece illustrated at the left is an outstanding example of the Egyptian sculptor's ability to represent realistically the poise of the human body in the course of movement. The pharaoh is about to harpoon a hippopotamus of Seth, the god of evil, which is not shown for magical reasons, because its presence in the tomb might be a source of danger to the king. (Cat. no. 35)

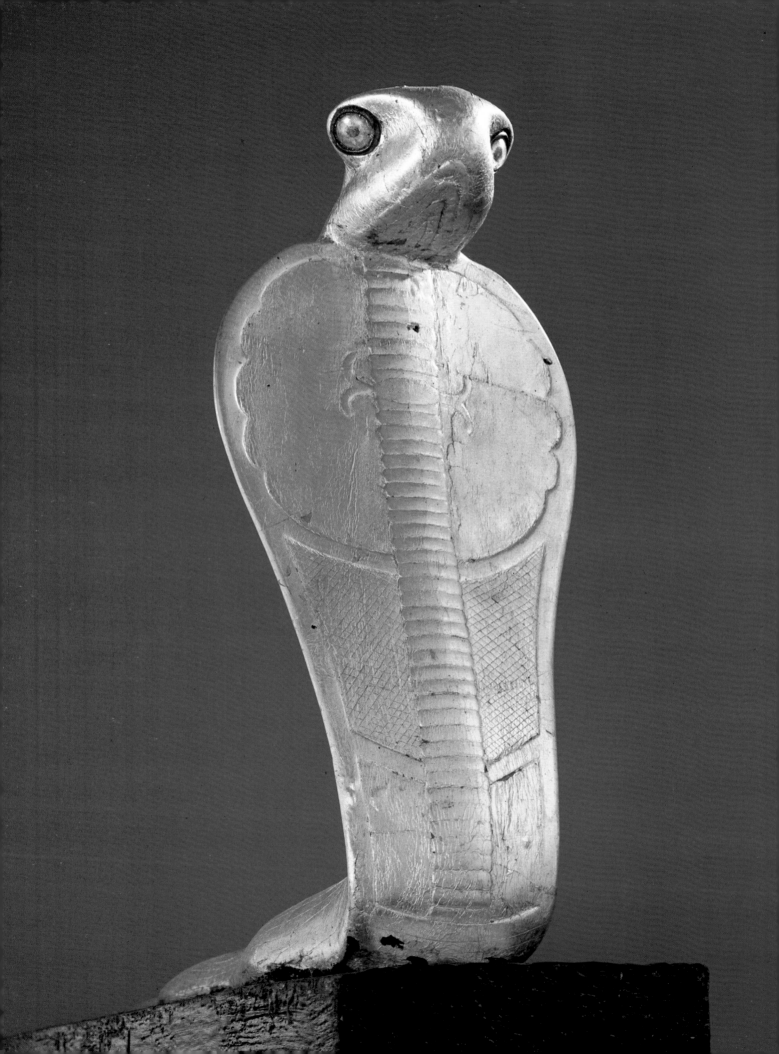

**PLATE 22** This dramatic creature is a cobra with dilated hood. Made of gilded wood, with quartz eyes, it represents a serpent deity that Tutankhamun believed would help him in the journey through the underworld. (Cat. no. 37)

Ptah, patron deity of artists and craftsmen, was the principal god of Memphis, the capital of Egypt in the time of the kings who built the pyramids. The theologians of Memphis maintained that it was Ptah who had created the world and all living creatures: his tongue uttered the name of everything and thereby brought it into existence. It was a more intellectual conception of the creation than the notion that the sun god emerged from a lotus, and it never lost its appeal to the Egyptians. (Cat. no. 39)

PLATE 23 Carved from a single piece of wood, this model consists of a figure of Tutankhamun wrapped in a shroud and lying on a bed. Beside the body are small figures of a falcon and a human-headed bird (called the *ba*-bird), each with one wing protectively laid on the body of the king; these are two of the forms that the king might adopt when visiting his body after it had been mummified. (Cat. no. 40)

*Shawabty* figures are among the commonest objects that have been preserved from ancient Egypt: they were substitutes for their deceased owner when the god Osiris ordered him to do manual labor in the next world. (Cat. no. 42)

**PLATE 24** This graceful figure portrays the goddess Selket, whose emblem, a scorpion, is placed on her head. She is one of four goddesses who stood outside the gilded wooden shrine that housed the chest containing Tutankhamun's mummified internal organs, the goddesses' outstretched arms spreading protection over their charges. Selket's divine role was not limited to funerary duties: also associated with childbirth and nursing, she was chiefly noted for her control of magic. (Cat. no. 43)

**PLATE 25** In its naturalistic style the statue of Selket resembles the art of
Amarna, but its most striking feature is the turn of the head sideways. It is the more
remarkable because it breaks one of the most fundamental and persistent
rules of Egyptian plastic art, the so-called rule of frontality, which meant every
figure carved in the round was supposed to face the viewer directly. (Cat. no 43)

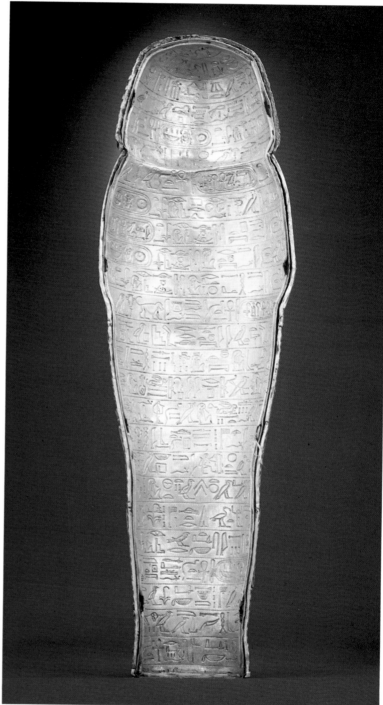

**PLATES 26 AND 27 (OVERLEAF)** This is one of
four miniature coffins that contained Tutankhamun's internal organs. Made of beaten gold inlaid
with colored glass and carnelian, the coffins may
originally have been made for Smenkhkara,
Akhenaton's co-regent at the end of his reign; there
is a general facial resemblance to Tutankhamun,
who was perhaps Smenkhkara's brother or half-
brother. (Cat. no. 45)

PLATE 28 The left paw of the lion depicted on this alabaster unguent vase rests on the hieroglyphic symbol for "protection." When the vase was found the crown was missing, having been wrenched off by ancient thieves. The contents, some dried fatty substance black in color, remained intact. (Cat. no. 53)

In the intricacy of its decoration, the angular bow shown in the detail below is one of the most elaborate of some fifty weapons of its class found in Tutankhamun's tomb. The head of the horse represented here is adorned with ostrich plumes, and an ostrich-plume fan is shown behind its flank. (Cat. no. 55)

PLATE 29 This ivory headrest has no close parallel in Egyptian art. Shu, god of the air, holds the curved support for the head. According to legend Shu brought chaos to an end, at the creation of the universe, by raising the sky high above the earth; this action had to be maintained continuously, for otherwise the sky would fall and chaos would return. To indicate that the base of the headrest represents the earth, the artist has included two lions, symbolizing the mountains on the eastern and western horizons between which the sun rose and set. (Cat. no. 48)

**PLATE 30** These two pieces reflect, in different ways, artistic interests of Tutankhamun's period. The vase above is made of silver – very rare in Egypt – and depicts a pomegranate, introduced from western Asia and probably still a prized novelty (Cat. no. 50). The elegant flask at the right is made of the finest alabaster, and is a product of a notable revival of the art of carving stone vessels that had been an outstanding achievement of early Egyptian craftsmen (Cat. no. 47).

PLATE 31  The principal decoration of the stool at the left is made up of the hieroglyphic sign for "unification" to which are tied stems of lotus and papyrus flowers, symbolizing the union of Upper and Lower Egypt. (Cat. no. 49)

The scepter at the right is made of sheet gold beaten on a wooden core, with a shaft in the form of a papyrus flower and stem. (Cat. no. 52)

The gameboard below is the largest of four found in Tutankhamun's tomb. To judge from the number of boards buried with him, the game must have been one of his favorite pastimes, and it also was described in the Book of the Dead as one of the occupations of the deceased person in the next world. (Cat. no. 46)

**PLATE 32** Vessels in the shape of animals and birds were made early in Egypt's history, but subsequently they seem to have gone out of fashion until the Eighteenth Dynasty. This ibex is carved of alabaster, but the horns — only one of which was found — are real animal's horns. The body was hollowed out to hold unguents. (Cat. no. 54)

Both artistically and technically this wooden chest is undoubtedly one of the most important works of art in the tomb of Tutankhamun. Carved and painted ivory panels depict Tutankhamun and his queen in gracious scenes reminiscent of much of the art of the preceding Amarna period. The sides are decorated with floral motifs and spirited animals. (Cat. no. 51)

**PLATE 33** In this delightful panel from the top of the painted chest, Tutankhamun is handed two bouquets by his wife, her bearing erect and yet graceful and mobile. (Cat. no. 51)

# CATALOGUE

I. E. S. EDWARDS
*Former Keeper of Egyptian Antiquities*
*British Museum*

*The objects are listed in the order
in which they were excavated.*

ENTRANCE PASSAGE

# 1
## THE SUN GOD ON A LOTUS
## COLOR PLATE 1

In remote antiquity, before Egypt had become a nation, the individual communities that inhabited the Nile Valley and the Delta developed their own conceptions of the origin of existence, some of which survived in historical times and are preserved either in religious texts or in pictorial reproductions, and frequently in both. These conceptions, having evolved independently, differed widely and they were never reduced to a single, universally accepted creed, although Akhenaton endeavored to bring about such a change immediately before the time of Tutankhamun. In one fundamental respect, however, there was a very considerable measure of agreement: before the first act of creation there was nothing but a watery abyss, the primordial ocean called Nun.

Nature had provided a parallel to the primordial ocean in the annual inundation of the country by the Nile, and just as mounds appeared above the water when the Nile flood began to recede, so, according to some of the most commonly held beliefs, the earth emerged initially, as a "High Mound," from the primordial ocean. Exactly where in Egypt this mound appeared was never decided: Hermopolis, Memphis, Heliopolis, and, later, Thebes (in the precincts of the temple of Medinet Habu) were all regarded by their respective theologians as the actual site of the primeval "High Mound." Once cosmic matter had evolved, creation could begin, first with the gods and then with all living creatures, including man.

One of the most picturesque explanations of the initial creation postulated that a lotus grew in a pool left by the receding waters and from the flower the sun god emerged as the first living being. A text dating from a later period describes the sun god as "He who emerged from the lotus upon the High Mound, who illumines with his eyes the Two Lands."

Elsewhere the lotus is sometimes represented not as the vehicle from which the sun god came into being but as a single entity with the god; a text in Berlin, dating from about two centuries after the time of Tutankhamun, calls the sun god "the great lotus who appeared from Nun."

This painted wooden figure clearly represents the infant sun god at the moment of birth emerging from the blue lotus. The features are unmistakably those of Tutankhamun. According to the solar creed, a king after death was identified with the sun god and consequently it was not uncommon to depict the sun god with the features of a particular king. One of the best-known examples is the giant sphinx at Giza, which represents the sun god in the form of a human-headed lion, and the face is thought to be a likeness of King Chephren in whose pyramid complex it stands.

In representing Tutankhamun in this fashion, the artist was not trying to convey the idea that the sun god when he came into being resembled Tutankhamun. There were several different schools of thought about what happened to the sun when it set every evening on the western horizon, and one theory was that the sun god, manifest in the sun, died at sunset to be reborn on the next morning in the lotus, thus repeating every day the the original creation. According to this theory, the earth was surrounded by the primordial ocean and floated on the surface of the ocean. By having this model in his tomb, Tutankhamun, through the process of imitative magic, would have an instrument that would enable him to be reborn as the sun god every day.

As a work of art this piece is one of the most outstanding in the whole contents of the tomb. In shape the elongated skull is very reminiscent of the representations of the Amarna princesses who may have been Tutankhamun's half-sisters. The face is that of a child, as would be expected in this context, though the perforation of the lobes of the ears seems an incongruous detail in a newly born child (see No. 29). It is carved in wood and overlaid with painted gesso, the eyebrows and eyelashes being blue in imitation of lapis lazuli, of which the sun god's hair was believed to be made (see No. 25).

This piece was not found in the chambers of the tomb but on the floor of the entrance corridor, under the rubble filling introduced by the necropolis staff after the first robbery. Since it is unlikely that it was accidentally dropped there when the furniture was placed in the tomb at the time of the funeral, it must be assumed that it was removed from the tomb by the first robbers and discarded on their way out.

*Cairo No. 60723; Carter No. 8.*
*Height 11¹³⁄₁₆ in. (30.0 cm.).*
*Carter III, pl. I; Desroches-Noble-*
*  court 294, frontispiece; Fox pl. 2;*
*  S. Morenz and J. Schubert 50.*
*Exhibitions: None.*

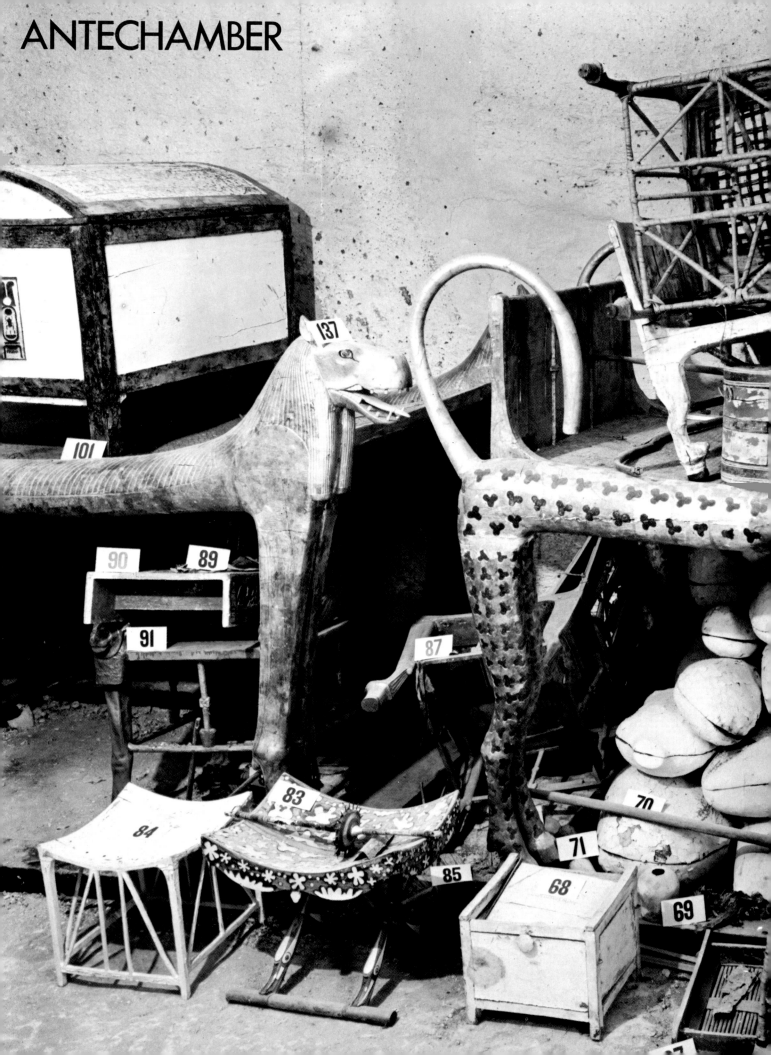

# 2
## WHITE LOTUS CHALICE
## COLOR PLATE 2

Carved of a single piece of alabaster (calcite) and inlaid with blue pigment, this chalice represents a single bloom of the white lotus (*Nymphaea lotus*), the characteristics of which, apart from its color, are sixteen to twenty ovoid petals and four ovoid sepals. In this piece sixteen petals are shown, all carved in very delicate relief. Rising from the base are two supports for the handles, each support consisting of a single flower of the blue lily (*Nymphaea caerulea*) and two buds. The petals and sepals of the blue lilies are narrow and pointed, while the number of petals in the flower is no more than twelve to sixteen. The handles, which are attached to the flowers and to the sides of the chalice, are composed of figures of Heh, the god of eternity, kneeling on the emblem of infinity and holding in each hand a palm rib (the hieroglyphic sign for "year") resting on a tadpole (see No. 10) and the

sign for "life" *(ankh)*.

Two inscriptions testify that Tutankhamun was the owner of the chalice. In the frame on the front are his throne name and his personal name with the appropriate titles and the epithet "Beloved of Amen-Ra, Lord of the Thrones of the Two Lands and Lord of Heaven, given life for ever." On the lip of the chalice the band of inscription is divided into two, one reading to the right from the center of the front and the other to the left; to the right: "May [he] live, the Horus 'Strong Bull, beautiful of birth,' the Two Ladies 'Goodly of Laws, who pacifies the Two Lands,' the Horus of Gold 'Exalted of Crowns, who placates the gods,' King of Upper and Lower Egypt and Lord of the Two Lands Nebkheperura, given life." To the left: "May your ka [spirit] live and may you spend millions of years, you who love Thebes, sitting with your face to the north wind, your two eyes beholding happiness."

The chalice was found just inside the door of the tomb, whither it had been taken by the robbers,

probably from the Annex. Its discoverers called it the "wishing cup," from the wish at the end of the inscription. Cups and chalices in the form of the flower of a lily and dating from the Eighteenth to the Twenty-second Dynasty are not uncommon; a small faience plaque in the Eton College collection actually shows Tutankhamun in the act of drinking from a large lotus chalice comparable in size with the present piece, but without handles. From the evidence at present available, it appears that the cups representing the white lotus were used as drinking vessels, whereas those representing the blue lily were used only for ritualistic purposes.

*Cairo No. 62125; Carter No. 14.*
*Height 7 3⁄16 in. (18.3 cm.), width 11 1⁄8 in. (28.3 cm.), depth of cup 6 5⁄8 in. (16.8 cm.).*
*Carter I, 110, 190, pl. XLVI; Desroches-Noblecourt 64, 299, pl. XXII B.*
*Exhibitions: Paris No. 42; London No. 7; U.S.S.R. No. 41.*

# 3
# TRUMPET
## COLOR PLATE 8

This trumpet, made of bronze or copper with gold overlay, is one of three known examples of the instrument preserved from ancient Egypt, two of which were found in the tomb of Tutankhamun; the third is in the Louvre. The bell is decorated with incised figures of the king and of three gods, all standing under the hieroglyphic sign for heaven: Ra-Harakhty (falcon-headed), Amen-Ra, and Ptah (mummified within a shrine and holding three scepters). With the trumpet is a wooden stopper to fit the tube and bell, almost certainly either for use with a cloth as a cleaner or to prevent the instrument being damaged and thus losing its shape when not in use. A hole at the thinner end of the stopper was probably intended for a thong by which it could be suspended beneath the arm from the shoulder while the trumpet was being blown. The bell is painted to resemble a lotus flower.

In comparison with a modern trumpet, this instrument is short and has no valves. The mouthpiece is a cylindrical sleeve with a silver ring at the outer end fixed to the outside of the tube; it is not cup-shaped or detachable. Both this trumpet and its companion in the tomb, which is made of silver, have been played in recent times and the lowest notes that could be clearly sounded were D and C respectively. Plutarch (*De Iside et Osiride* 30) remarked that the people of Busiris and Lycopolis did not use trumpets because they sounded like the braying of an ass, the ass being identified with the god Seth, the murderer of Osiris. It has been stated (H. Hickman, *La Trompette dans l'Egypte ancienne*, p. 1) that the trumpet is the only ancient instrument of which the exact sound, as heard by the ancients, can be reproduced today.

Several scenes in tombs and temples illustrate the trumpet in use and in most instances it is associated with military activities — processions of soldiers, battle scenes, and so forth. A trumpeter and a standard bearer are shown among the first Egyptian soldiers to scale the walls of an Asiatic town in a famous battle scene in the temple of Ramesses III at Medinet Habu (western Thebes). Sometimes a pair of trumpeters is shown, but it is noticeable that they are never represented both playing at the same time. As a rule, when he accompanied soldiers the trumpeter marched outside the column, punctuating by staccato notes the step of the soldiers.

It is impossible to be certain whether Tutankhamun's trumpets were intended solely for military purposes. Nevertheless the figures of the gods on the bell would suggest such a use, for these three gods were the tutelary deities of three out of four divisions of the army of Ramesses II at the battle of Qadesh (about 1275 B.C.), only about seventy-five years after Tutankhamun's death. Their names and epithets are written in hieroglyphs above the figures. The king's name is also given. On his head he wears the blue crown (*khepresh*), while in his left hand he holds a *heqat* scepter, of the same kind as No. 5, and the Egyptian sign for "life" (*ankh*). In addition to the helmet he wears a bead collar, a shrine-shaped pectoral suspended from his neck, and a pleated kilt with an animal's tail at the back. His feet are bare. The god standing in front of him, Amen-Ra, holds the sign for "life" to the king's nostrils and places the other hand on the king's shoulder.

This trumpet was found in a long chest in the Antechamber. It may have been taken there by the robbers from the Burial Chamber. The other trumpet, wrapped in a reed cover, was left in the southeast corner of the Burial Chamber outside the outermost golden shrine; it was made of silver.

*Cairo No. 62008; Carter No. 50 gg.*
*Length 19⁷⁄₁₆ in. (49.4 cm.), max.*
*diameter 3¾ in. (9.5 cm.).*
*Carter II, 19, pl. II B; Desroches-*
*Noblecourt 66; H. Hickman 17-19.*
*Exhibitions: Paris No. 39; London*
*No. 45; U.S.S.R. No. 24.*

## 4
## LEOPARD'S HEAD
## COLOR PLATE 3

One of the most important episodes in the funeral of an ancient Egyptian was the performance of a ceremony called "Opening the Mouth," the purpose of which was to restore life to the mummified body. It was performed outside the tomb by priests, at least one of whom, the *setem* priest, wore a leopard-skin mantle that covered most of the otherwise bare upper part of his body and extended downward over his skirt. It was worn in such a way that the head of the leopard fell over the priest's chest.

This episode is depicted in a painting on the north wall of Tutankhamun's burial chamber. The ritual is being performed on his mummy, which has been bandaged and clothed to resemble the god Osiris, and the officiant is King Ay, who had already succeeded to the throne as the *khepresh* crown (see No. 17) on his head shows. He wears the leopard-skin mantle and is clearly acting as the *setem* priest. In this particular ritual the *setem* priest represented both the son of the dead person and Horus the son of Osiris. Tutankhamun had no son but, having died, he had become identified with Osiris and his successor was identified with Osiris's

son Horus, although in this instance Ay would have been old enough to have been Tutankhamun's grandfather.

Leopard-skin mantles were worn by many categories of priests, besides the *setem*, when they were performing their sacerdotal duties. The origin and significance of the custom are unknown, but it was apparently regarded as a barbarous practice by Akhenaton, because the skin has been deliberately excised by the adherents of the Aton cult from the wall paintings in a number of Theban tombs dating from the pre-Amarna period. Its presence in the painting in Tutankhamun's tomb shows how completely the creed of his predecessor had been discarded.

Perhaps even more indicative of Tutankhamun's own disregard for Akhenaton's proscriptions was the fact that two "leopard skins" were included among articles of apparel buried with him, both packed tightly with a mass of other material in chests, where they had been hastily placed by the staff of the necropolis after the robberies, and both in a very poor state of preservation. One of the "skins" was only an imitation

made of cloth that, according to Carter, was decorated with tapestry-woven designs. The other, to which this head belonged, was a real leopard skin. The head, however, is not real; it is made of wood covered with gesso and overlaid with gold. The eyes are made of translucent quartz with the details painted at the back, while all the other inlaid features, including the king's cartouche with his throne name on the brow, are made of colored glass.

More than one reason can be suggested to account for the inclusion of these "leopard skins" in the tomb equipment. Perhaps the least probable is that a leopard skin would be needed by the king in the next life when he sailed across the sky to join the sun god, Ra, on the eastern horizon. In an allusion to this celestial journey, the ancient texts inscribed on the walls of the pyramids of the Fifth and Sixth Dynasties attribute these words to a deceased king: "My leopard skin is on my arm, my scepter is in my hand." It seems more likely, however, that Tutankhamun's leopard skins were buried with him because, in theory, each Egyptian king was the high priest of every god, and the official high priest was merely his deputy. The skins would thus have belonged to Tutankhamun's wardrobe for use on occasions when he was acting as a priest.

Carter states that the leopard's spots on the imitation skin were

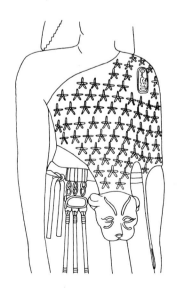

represented by hollow five-pointed stars made of sheet gold. In the case of the real leopard skin, such imitations of the spots would have been unnecessary, and yet some reddish gold stars and a gold cartouche inscribed with Tutankhamun's throne name had been attached to it, but the original positions of most of the stars on the mantle could not be determined. They were of two kinds: one kind was a simple five-pointed star (the only kind represented on the imitation "skin") and the other was a five-pointed star within a ring.

Isolated representations of each kind of star, but not on the same mantle, are known. The drawing at lower left depicts a statue of Queen Teye's brother, named Onen, in the Turin Museum that shows him wearing a leopard skin decorated with five-pointed stars and a cartouche inscribed with the throne name of Amenhotpe III, Teye's husband. Onen was a priest of Amun and a "Chief of Seers" of Heliopolis of Upper Egypt (Thebes); his starred leopard skin was doubtless his vestment in his latter capacity. In earlier times, "Chief of Seers" was the title of the high priest of the ancient temple of Heliopolis, near Cairo, probably because one of his duties consisted of observing the movements of the stars, and the leopard skin with stars was his mantle of office. In the Eighteenth Dynasty, when Thebes became the Heliopolis of Upper Egypt, the adoption of the title and the mantle by the priests followed naturally. Tutankhamun added the epithet "Ruler of Heliopolis of Upper Egypt" to his name when he became king, thereby emphasizing his devotion to the Heliopolitan cult. By virtue of being king he was also high priest of Heliopolis, and consequently he would have been entitled to wear the starred leopard skin.

A leopard skin with five-pointed stars within rings is depicted in a tomb at Thebes. It is worn by a high priest of the mortuary cult of the deceased king Thutmose I, named Userhat, who was in office about forty

years after the death of Tutankhamun. In addition to the stars, it is adorned with cartouches, those of Sethy I, no doubt because Userhat was acting as the king's deputy. Another example occurs in the tomb of a priest of the mortuary cult of Amenhotpe I, also at Thebes. Perhaps the stars in these instances are in rings because Tuthmose I and Amenhotpe I had gone to the underworld, a ringed star being the hieroglyphic sign for the underworld.

Although these representations show that leopard skins with one or

the other of the two kinds of stars were worn by certain priests, Tutankhamun's mantle with a mixture of ringed and unringed stars appears to be without parallel.

*Cairo No. 62629; Carter No. 44 q.*
*Height 6⅞ in. (17.5 cm.), width 6⅝ in. (16.9 cm.), max. thickness 1⁵⁄₁₆ in. (3.3 cm.).*
*Carter I, 113; E. Scamuzzi pl. XXXVI; N. de G. Davies pls. V-VIII, XI, XXIII.*
*Exhibitions: None.*

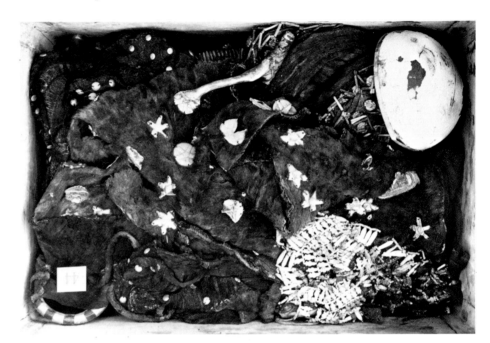

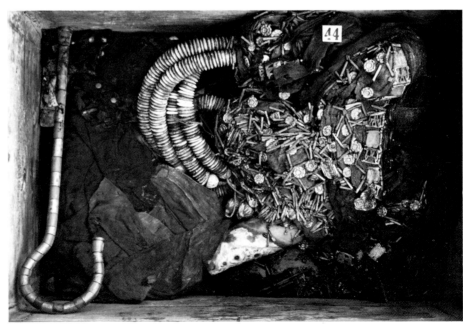

*Two stages in unpacking the box containing Cat. no. 4*

**5**
**CROOK AND FLAIL**
**COLOR PLATE 5**

These emblems were found separately, the crook in the Antechamber and the flail in the Treasury. The flail is historically the more interesting because it bears on the gold cap at the base of its handle the king's name in its early form of Tutankhaton together with his throne name Nebkheperura, thus showing that it had belonged to him while he was still a child, but after he had ascended the throne. Since a flail was one of

the symbols held by Egyptian kings in some of their coronation ceremonies, it is at least possible that this object was the actual flail used by Tutankhaton in his coronation at Amarna when he was about nine years of age and before he was crowned at Karnak. The crook is inscribed on both the terminal caps with the throne name only — a difference that, in spite of the equality in size of the two objects, may indicate that they were not originally made as a pair. A second pair and an odd crook, all larger, were found in the same wooden box as this flail. All three crooks are composed of alternating cylindrical sleeves of metal overlaid with gold and dark blue glass upon a bronze core. The handle of the flail, as far as the angular sleeve at the top, is similarly composed, but the gilded beads in the thongs of the swingle have wooden cores.

Although the crook and the flail were most often represented as emblems of the god Osiris, they were also carried on some ceremonial occasions, besides the coronation, by the reigning pharaoh. Very occasionally the crook was held by viceroys of Nubia and also by viziers. A painted scene of tribute from Asia in the tomb of Tutankhamun's viceroy of Nubia, Huy, shows the king holding both the crook and flail in his left hand and the sign for "life" *(ankh)* in his right, while the viceroy holds a crook, but no flail, in his left hand and a single ostrich plume (see No. 18) in his right. Only rarely is the flail shown in the hands of priests or officials and such instances are limited to scenes of royal jubilee festivals. Notwithstanding these sporadic exceptions, the crook and the flail were essentially Osirian emblems, though possibly not so in origin. Osiris is believed to have acquired them from Andjeti, the local god of a town in the Delta named Djedu, who was represented in human form with two feathers on his head and holding the crook and flail in his hands. At a very early date in Egyptian history Osiris absorbed Andjeti and

adopted his insignia. Osiris, however, was regarded not only as a god but also as a deified deceased king and consequently his insignia, particularly the crook and flail, were treated as symbols of royalty.

It is not difficult to imagine how a shepherd's crook could have acquired the symbolical significance of rulership. Its name in Egyptian is *heqat* and the most common word for "ruler" is *heqa*. Not unnaturally it has been compared with the crosier, the Christian pastoral staff. A flail (called *nekhakha*), however, seems out of character for a kindly and beneficent god like Osiris and for this reason some authorities prefer to regard it as a *ladanisterion*, a flail-like instrument used until the present day by shepherds in the Mediterranean region and elsewhere for collecting ladanum, a gummy substance excreted from the leaves of the *Cistus* plant. According to classical writers, it was used in the preparation of incense and unguents. This suggestion, proposed by the late Professor P. E. Newberry who helped in the clearance of Tutankhamun's tomb, is plausible, but, as yet, there is no clear evidence that the *Cistus* plant grew in Egypt in pharaonic times.

*Crook: Cairo No. 61759; Carter No. 44 u.*
*Lengths 13³⁄₁₆ in. (33.5 cm.).*
*Carter I, pl. XXIII A; III, 77-8, pl. XXI A; Desroches-Noblecourt 86, 179, fig. 104; P. E. Newberry 84-94.*
*Exhibitions: U.S.A. Nos. 4-5; Japan Nos. 4-5; Paris No. 17; London No. 44; U.S.S.R. No. 18.*

**6**
**OPENWORK BUCKLE**
**COLOR PLATE 5**

Tutankhamun is portrayed on this buckle as a warrior returning from battle in his chariot (see No. 55), with his hound running alongside. In front of the chariot are a bearded Asiatic and a Nubian — captives shackled together with stems of single flowers of a papyrus and a lily. It is simply a heraldic device, without historical foundation, for Tutankhamun himself probably never took part in any military exploit; even if he had done so, western Asia lay to the northeast of Egypt and Nubia to the south, so that a campaign against the peoples of both regions simultaneously would have been geographically impossible. The heraldic nature of the presentation is emphasized by the other elements in the composition: the protecting vulture of Hierakonpolis (Upper Egypt) hovering above the horses and extending the sign of "life" *(ankh)* toward the king; its counterpart, the winged serpent of Buto (Lower Egypt) with its wings outstretched behind him, embracing a cartouche bearing his throne name; and the cluster of papyrus growing in a swamp (see No. 10). Immediately behind the chariot is the formal inscription reading, "May all protection of life attend him like Ra for ever." In order to fill the bow-shaped space between the base of the buckle and the level ground beneath the chariot and horses, the artist has employed the standard motif symbolizing the unification of the Two Lands (see No. 49) in one of its many variants: the hieroglyph for "unification" *(sema)* is in the center and bound to it by lotus and papyrus stems are a Nubian and an Asiatic captive, the whole group being flanked by a lily symbolizing Upper Egypt on the right and a papyrus flower and buds for Lower Egypt on the left. Interpreted baldly, the device would mean that Tutankhamun, protected by the goddesses of Upper and Lower Egypt and supported by the inhabitants of Upper and Lower Egypt, will vanquish all his enemies.

If this buckle be compared with the scene on the reverse side of the ostrich-feather fan, No. 18, it will be evident that the king's equipment on his return from battle was the same as it was after hunting. In each case he wears the short wig and long pleated robe, though both in the hunt depicted

on the fan and in the battle scenes on the famous painted casket found in his tomb he wears a leopard-skin corselet and a kilt with apron. The trappings of the horses are very similar, though not identical; on the buckle, moreover, there is no visible connection between the reins and the bit. The hound, wearing the customary broad collar, also figures in the hunt, and a pair of hounds accompany the king in the battle scenes on the casket. In only one respect is there a marked difference between the accessories shown on the three objects: most of the accouterments on the buckle are more richly decorated — in particular, the king's wig and elaborate collar, the chariot, the collar of the hound, and the housing and harness of the only horse that can can be completely seen are all edged with applied gold granules.

The sheet gold of which this buckle is made shows the reddish or rose-pink color that is common to very many of the gold objects found in Tutankhamun's tomb. It is not an indication of some natural impurity in the metal; it is a film so thin that measurement is difficult, but it is believed to be less than one hundred-thousandth of an inch in thickness and to have been produced by a process using either iron oxide or iron pyrites and soda.

Egyptian artists tried to avoid intersecting the human body or any part of it by interposing between it

and the viewer objects that must have lain between them in reality. Three of the objects discussed in this volume show the king drawing his bow (Nos. 13, 18, and 51) — an action that could only be performed effectively by placing the arrow close to the neck and having the lower half of the bow-string crossing the body diagonally, but the artist has adopted a different technique in each instance. In the scene on this buckle the king holds a pair of reins in each hand and, in addition, his bow in his left hand and his whip in his right, but no part of the hand or arm is obscured by the objects carried. The same reluctance to screen one object with another is shown in the representation of the bow case, the lower end of which passes between the spokes of the chariot wheel, although higher up the rim of the wheel cuts across the middle of the case. The hound — a strong, lithe animal — also is conventionally shown, his hind half behind the legs of the far horse and his head on the viewer's side of the near horse, as though his body stretched right across the bellies of the horses.

*Cairo No. 87847; Carter No. 44 (?; the location of this piece was not recorded).*
*Width 3⁵⁄₁₆ in. (8.5 cm.), height 2⁷⁄₁₆ in. (6.2 cm.).*
*Desroches-Noblecourt 98, pl. XXIIa, 299; Vilímková 64.*
*Exhibitions: None.*

## 7
## PORTABLE CHEST
## COLOR PLATE 7

Found on the floor of the Antechamber, this chest had been stripped of its original contents by the tomb robbers and refilled with vessels and a miscellaneous collection of other objects, including stone knives, the lid of a rush basket, lumps of resin, balls of incense, and dried fruits.

Both its gable lid and the box are made of ebony framework with recessed inner panels of red wood, probably cedar. The joints are either dovetail or mortise and tenon, the latter being secured by wooden pegs. As a border to each panel there are three or four contiguous strips of ivory and polished ebony veneer laid alternately. At the top of the box, projecting outward beyond the line of the lid, is a plain cavetto cornice with a gilded molding at the base. The feet are capped with bronze shoes and strengthened with bent right-angle braces; at the bottom of the walls, on the underside, are strips of ivory that follow the bends of the braces and fit into slots on the inner sides of the bronze shoes. Two gilded mushroom-shaped knobs, one on the lid and the other on an end panel, served as terminals for a tie that

could not be undone without breaking the seal covering the knot. Each knob bears within a shrine-shaped frame the cartouche of Tutankhamun mounted on the hieroglyphic sign for "gold" *(nub)* and flanked by uraei wearing either the double crown (left uraeus) or the crown of Lower Egypt (right uraeus). Both uraei have pendent life signs *(ankh)* at the base of their hoods.

Unlike the other chests found in the tomb, this chest, no doubt because of its size and weight when full, was provided with four poles so that it could be carried by bearers on their shoulders. Each pole slides backward and forward through two bronze rings, attached to boards fixed to the bottom of the box. A collar at the back end of the pole, greater in circumference than the ring, prevents the pole from slipping forward through the inner ring. When the chest was not being carried, the poles could be pushed back until the collars of two axially opposite poles were touching each other and the poles were then entirely concealed from view. Portable chests of this kind are represented in relief on the walls of the mastaba tombs of high officials, such as Mereruka and Ankhmahor at Sakkara, dating from about a thou-

sand years before the time of Tutankhamun. No other example of an actual portable chest is known.

Carved in low relief on one end of the chest within a rectangular frame, the top of which is in the form of the hieroglyphic sign for "heaven," are figures of the king and a god facing each other and separated by a vase on a stand. The king, whose ear is pierced for an earring (see No. 29), wears the blue crown (see No. 17) with uraeus and streamers, a broad collar and bracelets, and a kilt with apron. In his outstretched hands he offers the god a lamp and a pot of unguent. The lidded vase on the stand is of the same shape as some blue faience vessels found in the tomb, apart from the spout that, in this representation, is in the form of an ostrich feather signifying "truth, justice, right order" (*maat* – see No. 22). According to a hieratic inscription on the box containing those vessels, they were called by the name *nemset*, which must apply also to this vase, although its shape does not correspond exactly with that of *nemset* vases dating from earlier times. When figured in ritual scenes carved on temple walls, they contain cold water for libations. The god, called in the accompanying inscription "Onnophris, who is at the head of the West, the great god, Lord of the Necropolis," is only another form of Osiris. On his head he wears the *atef* crown with ostrich plumes and the uraeus. The artificial beard strapped to his chin is exceptionally

long and straight. His body, as regularly, is shrouded in a long white garment from which his hands protrude, one holding a long crook and the other a flail, the regular insignia of Osiris. Under his feet is a pedestal in the form of a hieroglyphic sign that has the same sound value and meaning as the ostrich feather. It is noticeable that the king is described in the hieroglyphic inscription as "the Osiris, Nebkheperura," which shows that the action which he was performing was conceived as taking place after his death.

The funerary character of the chest is further demonstrated by the inscriptions. Bands of text, incised and filled with yellow paint, on both the lid and box consist, in the main, partly of utterances by various deities and partly of offering formulae. The gods who deliver the utterances – Thoth, Geb, Harendotis, Harakhty, and Ptah-Soker-Osiris – promise the king among other things that his mouth, his eyes, and his ears will be opened, that his limbs will be rejuvenated, that heaven will receive his soul and earth his body, and that he will be granted all kinds of sustenance. In the offering formulae the gods – Geb, Harakhty-Atum, Osiris-Onnophris, and the divine Enneads – assure the king that, in return for the offerings presented to them, he will enjoy the sweet cool breeze, wine, and the odor of incense, he will assume, like the sun god, any form he chooses, he will be in the company of the gods in the bark of his father, Ra, he will be reborn daily like the sun, he will live as long as the sun and will be granted all the other benefits that can be accorded to a king when he is among the blessed dead.

Four columns of inscription at the gable ends of the lid name not only the king but also "the Great Royal Wife, his beloved, the Mistress of the Two Lands, Ankhesenamun."

*Cairo No. 61445; Carter No. 32.*
*Length 32¹¹/₁₆ in. (83.0 cm.), width*
*23¹³/₁₆ in. (60.5 cm.), height 25*
*in. (.63.5 cm.).*
*Carter I, 114, pls. XVI, XVII, LV;*
*Baker 94, fig. 115; Desroches-*
*Noblecourt 58.*
*Exhibitions: Paris No. 26; London*
*No. 14; U.S.S.R. No. 49.*

# 8
# CHILD'S CHAIR
# COLOR PLATE 6

Both in form and in construction this wooden chair is typical of its period. The curved back, set at a backward slant, is supported behind by three vertical stiles, one in the middle and one at each side, all joined to the toprail and the back of the frame of the seat. The five wooden slats of the seat are curved with a double cove and fastened to the sides of the frame by means of mortise and tenon joints reinforced by bronze or copper rivets capped with gold. Similar joints are used throughout. Curved wooden brackets overlaid with strips of ivory strengthen the base joints of the front uprights of the armrests and the two stiles on the flanks. The legs, shaped like a lion's paws with inlaid claws of ivory, stand on beaded drums shod with metal. Rounded stretchers, ornamented with papyrus-flower terminals of ivory and fixed to the middle of the legs, help to keep the chair rigid and serve as a base for the latticework bracing between them and the frame of the seat.

The wood is said to be ebony, a material that the Egyptians imported from Africa. The toprail and the back support are decorated with ivory marquetry of geometric designs broken by a frieze of single floral petals and lotus buds, which covers the upper crosspiece of the frame surrounding the back panel. The panel itself is overlaid on both its concave and convex faces with broad upright strips of ivory and ebony arranged alternately and separated by narrow borders of the same material. In contrast with this formal decoration the armrests have gilded panels adorned with scenes of a naturalistic kind. Although not absolutely identical in detail, the outer faces of the two panels show a recumbent ibex with

one front and one back hoof raised and its head turned back over its shoulder, and a desert plant within a border of continuous spirals. The inner faces are devoted to desert plants enclosed in a striated border.

Although the chair bears no inscription, its inclusion in Tutankhamun's tomb furniture leaves little room for doubt that it was made for him when he was a child. A chair almost identical in its overall dimensions was made for Satamun, a daughter of Amenhotpe III and Queen Teye, but its decoration was more elaborate and it was gilded, the whole appearance being more typical of a piece of royal furniture than Tutankhamun's chair. If they were brother and sister, as some authorities believe, the difference in richness would be unexpected.

*Cairo No. 62033; Carter No. 39.*
*Height 28 in. (71.12 cm.), width*
*14½ in. (36.83 cm.), depth 15½*
*in. (39.37 cm.).*
*Carter I, 114, pl. LIX; Baker, 84-6,*
*fig. 99; Singer, et al. I, 686*
*(fig. 485 B).*
*Exhibitions: Paris No. 13; London*
*No. 16; U.S.S.R. No. 43.*

## 9
## PAINTED CASKET
## COLOR PLATE 7

When found, this alabaster casket was lying in the Antechamber with the lid removed, no doubt by the robbers. There was nothing to suggest that they had interfered with its contents, which consisted mainly of an ivory pomegranate (see No. 50), a layer of cloth, a mass of decayed (horse?) hair, and two balls of hair wrapped in linen, one 2 inches (5 cm.) and the other 2⅜ inches (6 cm.) in diameter. Balls of dried Nile mud, sometimes with tufts of hair in the center and sometimes with fragments of papyrus or linen, have been found in Egyptian tombs and they are thought to have had a magical significance, the nature of which is still obscure, although there is evidence to suggest that they were associated with some form of contract. Since this casket bears the names of both the king and the queen, it is conceivable that each ball contains the hair of one of them. If some contract of importance was thereby signified, it may explain why such simple articles were placed in so elaborate a casket.

The box and lid of this casket are each carved from a single piece of alabaster (calcite) and the two knobs are made of obsidian (volcanic glass). The decoration throughout is incised and filled with colored pigments. On the lid it consists of formal bouquets in which the chief components are a papyrus flower, cornflowers, mandrakes, and lily petals. Two identical horizontal bands of blue lily petals beneath friezes of a checker pattern decorate the box. At the head end the bands are broken by a rectangular frame within which are the cartouches of the king (left and center) and of the queen (right). Above the cartouches are their titles "Good God, Lord of the Two Lands" and "Son of Ra, Lord of the Diadems" for the king, and "Great Royal Wife" for the queen. The cartouches of the king are followed by the wish that he may be "given life for ever and ever" and beneath the cartouche

of the queen is the wish that she may "be given life and be fruitful."

*Cairo No. 61762; Carter No. 40.*
*Length 13 in. (33.0 cm.), width*
  *6¹¹⁄₁₆ (17.0 cm.), height 9⁷⁄₁₆ in.*
  *(24.0 cm.).*
*Carter I, 200, pl. LXVI A.*
*Exhibitions: U.S.A. No. 27; Japan*
  *No. 17; London No. 5; U.S.S.R.*
  *No. 47.*

## 10
## FLORAL UNGUENT VASE
## COLOR PLATE 5

Some fifty alabaster (calcite) vases for unguents were found in the tomb, nearly all of them emptied of their contents by thieves in a second visitation (the tomb had also been robbed in antiquity of objects made of precious metals). It has been estimated that the total quantity of unguent placed in the tomb amounted to about 105 U.S. gallons (400 liters). That the robbers should have risked their lives to obtain it and also that they should have chosen it in preference to the many other treasures at their mercy would alone prove that it was a costly commodity. The vases being heavy and, in the case of this vessel and four others of the same general character, too large to move through the tunnel, the robbers poured the precious oils into waterskins for removal. Chemical analysis of the contents of one of the vessels found intact showed that the principal constituent was animal fat, to which some resin or balsam had been added, while cedar oil was identified as the base ingredient of another specimen. The perfume was extracted from flowers, gum resins, and other fragrant substances by wringing them in cloths and squeezing out the odoriferous liquids.

Floral motifs, particularly representations of the papyrus and the lotus (or its variant, the lily), were often used to decorate Egyptian unguent vessels. The lotus was perhaps the most fragrant flower in the Nile Valley and therefore very appropriate for adorn-

*Alabaster vases stacked in the Antechamber; the vase described here (Cat. no. 10) is labeled "60"*

ing containers intended for sweet-smelling unguents. The papyrus, however, was almost odorless and its association with the lotus in this connection is probably the result of the regular juxtaposition of the two plants in sculpture and painting as the representative emblems of Lower Egypt (papyrus) and Upper Egypt (lotus). With their stems intertwined, as on the neck of this vase, they symbolized the union of the two divisions of the land at the beginning of the First Dynasty.

Carved of two blocks of alabaster of unequal height cemented together, this piece consists of a long-necked amphora and its stand, each flanked by symbols arranged symmetrically in an openwork design. On a level with the base of the vase and on the vase itself is a double row of triangular incisions indicating a papyrus swamp. At each end of the row is a figure of a tadpole mounted on a ring of rope; as a hieroglyphic sign the tadpole means "one hundred thousand" and the ring of rope "infinity," and combined in this fashion the two signs mean "one hundred thousand times infinity." The notched stems above this group, which form the outermost elements in the handles of the vase, represent palm ribs, the hieroglyphic sign for "year." Between the palm ribs and the vase are the stems and flowers of papyrus and lotus, either growing from the swamp or tied to the neck of the vase by the so-called magical knot. On the front of the neck, carved in relief, is the head of the goddess Hathor; attached to her collar, which is incised and filled with a black pigment, is a lotus flower flanked by two buds and beneath it a single mandrake fruit. On the belly of the vase, under a frieze of petals, are representations of two human breasts and the names and titles of Tutankhamun, in part written defectively.

The stand consists of a central support flanked by two signs of "life" *(ankh)*, the crosspieces of which are in the form of human arms and hands, each holding the hieroglyph for "dominion" *(was)*. The inner hands also hold single papyrus flowers and stems which extend to the central support.

*Cairo No. 62118; Carter No. 60. Height 19 11/16 in. (50.0 cm.). Carter I, pl. XXII; Fox pl. 13. Exhibitions: Paris No. 36; London No. 3; U.S.S.R. No. 40.*

## 11
## MODEL FOLDING STOOL
## COLOR PLATE 3

In the time of Tutankhamun a woman might sit on a chair, a rigid stool (see No. 49), or even on a hassock (see No. 13) but, to judge from scenes painted on the walls of tombs, not on a folding stool; it seems to have been a male prerogative. Many examples of such stools have been found, two in the tomb of Tutankhamun with fragments of leather seats still adhering to their upper crossbars.

This stool, having an inflexible seat that is firmly joined to the legs, is in reality rigid, but it is an imitation of a folding stool with a leopardskin seat. Leopards were already extinct in Egypt in the New Kingdom, but skins of the beast were regularly included among the objects sent annually from Nubia as tribute to the reigning pharaoh. Organizing the collection and despatch of this tribute was one of the duties of the Egyptian viceroy of Nubia. Tutankhamun's viceroy of Nubia was a person named Huy, and in his tomb at Thebes there is a scene of himself accompanied by Nubian princes presenting their tribute to Tutankhamun, one of the objects being a folding stool with a seat of leopard skin.

The African leopard's skin being buff color, it is perhaps strange that the seat of this stool should have been carved in ebony, a black material; the markings are made of ivory inlay and are therefore light in color, the result being a reversal of the contrast in nature. Nevertheless, the pattern of the markings, as a mixture of spots and hollow rosettes, is fairly true to nature, though somewhat stylized. The tail, hanging down from one end of a narrow strip of red wood running along the middle of the seat and probably representing the backbone, is disproportionately short in relation to the length of the skin; the ivory inlay at the tip, marked with longer hairs, is peculiar. Probably the four paws were represented on the overhang at the corners of the stool but

*The model folding stool (Cat. no. 11) as it was found, in front of the animal-shaped couches in the Antechamber*

were wrenched off by the robbers, leaving visible scars, because the claws were made of gold. Fortunately the handsome gold bands with decorated rings on the legs and at the ends of the bottom bars were left untouched, as were the two gold caps covering the ends of the pivotal pins.

If the four feet were placed at the corners of the seat, it would explain why the legs, which are also made of ebony with ivory inlay, are not those of a leopard but are in the form of ducks' necks and heads, holding the crossbars in their bills. The stool in Huy's tomb has legs representing a leopard's paws, which would seem more natural to us. Ducks' heads and necks were, however, so commonly reproduced in the design of folding stools that the ancient Egyptians would not have been conscious of any incongruity in this combination of bird and mammal elements. Indeed, it may be regarded as evidence that the stool was made in Egypt from materials (probably including the gold) brought from Nubia, rather than that it came ready-made with a delivery of tribute.

*Cairo No. 62035; Carter No. 83.*
*Height 13⁹/₁₆ in. (34.5 cm.).*
  *Seat: length 18⁵/₁₆ in. (46.5 cm.),*
  *width 11¹³/₁₆ in. (30.0 cm.).*
  *Base: length 15¾ in. (40.0 cm.),*
  *width 12⅜ in. (31.5 cm.).*

*Carter I, 119, 218, pl. LXXIV B;*
  *Baker 87-9, fig. 102; Desroches-*
  *Noblecourt 198-9, fig. 117.*
*Exhibitions: None.*

## 12
## CEREMONIAL CHAIR
## COLOR PLATE 2

All the evidence suggests that this fine piece of furniture and the footstool found with it were intended for use by the king in a religious ceremony, probably at his coronation.

Although the chair is generally regarded as being made of cedar, there is reason to doubt whether the description is botanically correct. The wood, which is reddish in color, is strong, finely grained, and perfect in texture. It is certainly not a native product. From very early times Egypt imported timber from Lebanon, whose so-called cedars are mentioned in the Old Testament in connection with the building operations of David and Solomon. Very probably this chair is made of that same wood, but, if it has been correctly identified as belonging to a coniferous species *Abies cilicica*, "Cilician fir," it is not botanically a true cedar.

The general design of the chair represents a style that, with variations in detail, is found on many monuments of the New Kingdom. Three examples can be seen on the golden

shrine (No. 13) and one on the ornamented chest (No. 51). The slatted seat, deeply curved with a double cove, is attached to the outer frame by mortise and tenon joints. Similar joints were used throughout and those that were subjected to the greatest strain were pegged with gold-capped dowels, probably made of bronze or copper. The lion-paw legs have ivory claws and each paw stands on a beaded drum that is sheathed with gold and shod with bronze. Of the gilded grille between the stretchers and the seat, only the central feature (the hieroglyphic sign for "unification") and the base elements of the lotus and papyrus plants have survived the destructive attentions of the robbers. When complete it must have resembled the grille on the white stool (No. 49). The sloping and slightly curved back support consists of a carved inner panel and an outer frame strengthened behind by three upright stiles fixed to the rear of the seat and to the top rail. Added firmness is given to the base joints at the sides of the back support and to the outer stiles by curved wooden brackets, overlaid with sheet gold ornamented with continuous spirals and the striated band found on Nos. 8 and 49.

Material and design both contribute to the impressiveness of the superbly carved elements of the inner panel. In the center is the god of eternity, Heh, represented in the classic pose, kneeling on the hieroglyphic sign for "gold" and grasping in each hand a notched palm rib attached at the base to a tadpole mounted on the sign for "infinity" (see Nos. 10 and 19). At the top of each rib is a solar disk with pendent uraeus, from whose hood is suspended the "banner" engraved with the Horus name of Tutankhamun, "Strong Bull, beautiful of birth," surmounted by the falcon of Horus, also with uraeus, wearing the double crown of Upper and Lower Egypt. A large sign for "life" *(ankh)* hangs from the god's right arm. On his head is the solar disk flanked by uraei with "infinity" signs facing panels bearing the king's personal and throne names, each with its appropriate title and the regular formulae.

Every detail in this carving has been executed with the utmost feeling and delicacy. Each hieroglyphic sign is a work of art in itself and the figure of the god possesses elegance and grace. The setting, too, beneath the golden emblem of Horus of Behdet — the sun's disk with wings and pendent uraei — adds to the impressiveness of the composition. In all the surrounding inscriptions the emphasis is on the divine origin of the king and on his descent from the gods; they are thus in accord with the theme of the central feature. As an example, the inscription beginning in the middle of the top rail of the inner panel and running leftward can be translated: "May the good god live, the son of Amun, offspring of the majesty of Ra, excellent seed and pure egg, whom Horus nurtured in the temple [of Atum at Heliopolis], whose beauty the Souls of Heliopolis created and whom Atum caused to appear in glory on his throne, the King of Upper and Lower Egypt, Lord of the Two Lands, Nebkheperura, the Son of Ra, his beloved, Tutankhamun, Ruler of Heliopolis of Upper Egypt." The same sense, but in different words, is expressed in the other inscriptions carved on both the front and the back.

*Cairo No. 60708; Carter No. 29.*
*Height 37¾ in. (96.0 cm.), width 18⅞ in. (47.9 cm.), depth 20 1/16 in. (51.0 cm.).*
*Carter I, 116, pls. LX, LXI; Desroches-Noblecourt 69, pl. XIV; Baker 83, pls. 95, 96; Fox 17.*
*Exhibitions: Japan No. 43.*

# 13
## GOLDEN SHRINE
## COLOR PLATES 8-9

Some two thousand years before the time of Tutankhamun, the vulture goddess of Elkab, Nekhbet, was worshiped locally in an oblong pavilion made of a light wooden frame, the top of which was covered with the skin of an animal. The earliest representations, which date from about 3100 B.C., show this pavilion in a stylized form, sometimes mounted on a sledge, as in the drawing at the right. Its roof frequently has a hump at the front and a downward slope toward the back. It was called the Great House *(per wer)*. When the rulers of Elkab succeeded in establishing their supremacy over the whole of Upper Egypt and ultimately, through Menes, in conquering Lower Egypt, Nekhbet was promoted to the position of joint tutelary goddess of the king of the Two Lands, her partner being the serpent goddess of Buto, Wadjet, who had advanced from local to national recognition under the former kings of Lower Egypt. The sanctuaries of the two goddesses (called *iterty*) were then regarded as representative of the sanctuaries of all the local deities in their respective regions of the united kingdom. Thus, in the step pyramid enclosure of Djoser (about 2650 B.C.), two rows of dummy shrines faced each other in the jubilee festival court, one row for the gods of Upper Egypt in the form of the sanctuary of Nekhbet and the other row for the gods of Lower Egypt in the form of the sanctuary of Wadjet *(per nu)*.

Tutankhamun's small shrine is in the form of the sanctuary of Nekhbet mounted on a sledge. It is made of wood overlaid with a layer of gesso and covered with sheet gold. The wooden sledge is overlaid with silver. Carter was of the opinion that the gesso was first modeled in relief and the plain sheet gold was then pressed against it until it had regis-

tered the impression of the modeling, the outer face of the gold being finally chased. It seems doubtful, however, whether the gesso, even reinforced by gossamer-like linen, which a recent examination has shown to be present on both faces of the exposed gesso on the inside of one of the doors, would have had the strength to withstand the amount of pressure and friction involved in the process. If this doubt is valid, the scenes and inscriptions must have been worked on the gold itself; the gold sheets would then have been put face downward on a flat surface and covered with a piece of linen; the gesso in a liquid state would have been poured on the back of the linen so that it filled the depressions on the reverse side of the gold and, while it was still soft, the second piece of linen would have been applied to the outer surface. The purpose of the gesso would thus have been to give support to the decoration on the gold and to provide a flat surface for attachment to the wooden walls, roof, and door.

Every exposed surface of the shrine is covered with scenes, inscriptions, or some other kind of decoration, all in relief, of which the following are the principal:

*Roof:* Fourteen vultures of the goddess Nekhbet, with outstretched wings, are represented in relief on the top of the roof, seven on each side of a single column of inscription giving the names and titles of the king and queen. The vultures hold in their talons the hieroglyphic sign for "infinity" *(shen)*. Cartouches bearing the names of either the king or the queen occupy the space at each side of the talons. On the front of the roof is the winged disk of Horus of Behdet, the place being named in the inscriptions at the tips of the wings. A winged uraeus with the "infinity" sign between its wings occupies the entire length of each of the vertical sides of the roof.

*Front:* Beneath the roof on all four sides and projecting outward at the top is a cavetto cornice with a torus molding at the base. The whole of the front of the shrine is in the form of a doorway, the lintel of which is decorated with the winged disk of Horus of Behdet and the jambs bear inscriptions describing the king (left) as "the son of Ptah and Sekhmet," and (right) as "the image of Ra who does what is beneficial to him who begat him." In each case he is proclaimed as "beloved of [the goddess] Uret Hekau," a name meaning "The Great Enchantress," who is called in another inscription on the shrine "Lady of the Palace."

Each of the two doors is provided at the top and bottom with pivots,

*The contents of the shrine (Cat. no. 13); note the imprint of feet on the pedestal*

108

which fit into sockets, one in the lintel and the other in the floor of the sledge, and with a silver bolt that slides through two gold staples into a third staple in the other door. Two additional staples, side by side in the middle of each door, were intended for a sealed tie. On the outer faces of the door are representations of incidents in the daily life of the king and queen, arranged in three panels on each door. The uppermost panel on the left-hand door shows the queen in a plumed headdress standing with hands upraised before the king, who holds in his right hand the crook and scepter and in his left a lapwing. In the corresponding panel on the right-hand door and on both the middle panels, the queen holds out bunches of flowers toward the king and in the middle panel on the right she also holds a sistrum. The queen's headdress in two of these scenes is surmounted by a cone of unguent, flanked in one instance by uraei with the sun's disk. In the middle panels the king is seated on a stool (left) and on a chair (right), both with thick cushions. He wears the blue crown (see No. 17) on the left and the *nemes* headdress on the right. In the bottom panels, on the left side, the queen holds the king's arm with both hands and, on the right, the king's hand with her left hand, while extending a blue lotus and buds toward him in her right hand.

The gold overlay from the inner face of the left-hand door is lost, but it is evident from the damaged impression on the surviving gesso that its decoration was very similar to that of the right-hand door. Sandwiched between two panels that are entirely filled with the king's cartouches and supporting uraei is another scene of the queen holding a bunch of flowers and a sistrum toward the king. In this case her headdress is surmounted by lyriform horns and the sun's disk with two high plumes. At the bottom are two lapwings with outstretched human arms, both mounted on the hiero-

glyphic sign for "all" *(neb)* and having a five-pointed star *(dua)* beneath the arms, thus forming a kind of monogram meaning "adoration of all people."

*Sides:* The toprails and two stiles of both sides are inscribed with the names and titles of the king and queen, followed by the words "beloved of the Great Enchantress" with or without the epithet "Lady of the Palace."

On the left side, in the upper register, the king stands in a boat made of papyrus stems throwing a boomerang, but the quarry — wild fowl rising from the papyrus marshes — is not shown. The queen stands behind him as an onlooker; in her left hand she holds a flail or perhaps a fly whisk. The king, who wears a corselet on the upper part of his body and over it two representations of falcons, holds in his left hand four birds that may represent his "bag" or may be tame fowl used as decoys. In the clump of papyrus behind the prow of the boat can be seen a nest with two fledglings. The right-hand portion of this register is occupied with a scene that, although different in detail, repeats the theme of the bottom panel on the outside of the left-hand door. In the present setting it seems out of place.

A second fowling scene is represented in the lower register. The action is not conducted from a boat, but on the bank at the edge of a papyrus swamp. The king is seated on a stool with a thick cushion, his tame lion is by his side, and the queen squats on a cushion at his feet. Behind his head is the vulture of Nekhbet. He is in the act of shooting an arrow at birds rising from the swamp, one of which has already been hit. The string of his bow has been delineated by the artist as though it passed around the king's neck (see No. 6). His quiver hangs down behind him, suspended on a strap from his shoulder. As in the similar scene on the head end of the chest No. 51, the queen holds an arrow in her hand, ready to pass it to the king. With her other hand

she seems to be pointing at the fledglings in the nest, perhaps urging the king to take care not to hurt them.

The other (right) side has four scenes, all of an unusual kind. In the left of the top register the queen extends toward the king a sistrum and a necklace with an elaborate counterpoise. At the front of the counterpoise are the head and shoulders of a goddess, surmounted by cow's horns and the sun's disk and having the uraeus on her brow. Human hands project from beneath her collar, each hand holding a sign for "life" *(ankh)* toward the king. The identity of the goddess is revealed as the Great Enchantress in the inscription beneath the necklace. Addressing the king, the queen says: "Adoration in peace, receive the Great Enchantress, O Ruler, beloved of Amun!"

In the second scene in the top register the king, seated on a cushioned chair, holds out a vessel containing flowers and the queen pours water into the vessel from a vase in her right hand. In her left hand she holds a lotus flower and bud and a poppy.

On the left of the lower register the king pours water from a vessel into the cupped right hand of the queen. Her left elbow rests on his knee. The king, holding a bouquet of lotus flowers and poppies, sits on a stool covered with a cushion and an animal skin. What appear to be balls under the claw feet are in reality the ends of rounded crossbars. In the right-hand scene the queen is tying the king's floral collar behind his neck while he sits in a chair festooned with flowers. Nekhbet's vulture hovers over his head.

*Back:* Two scenes decorate the back. In the uppermost the queen stoops toward the king, her right hand touching his left arm. In her left hand she holds, in addition to a bunch of lotus flowers and buds hanging downward, an unguent-cone holder mounted on a stand and decorated with lotus flowers. A comparable scene on the back panel of the

# 108 C

*The Great Enchantress suckling Tutankhamun, found in the shrine (Cat. no. 13)*

form of a human-headed serpent suckling Tutankhamun: the accompanying inscription identifies the serpent as the Great Enchantress, who is mentioned ten times in the inscriptions on the outside of the shrine, once in connection with the necklace and elaborate counterpoise presented by the queen to the king. The goddess was thus associated with the king in a maternal capacity, but as a rule she is the uraeus that was placed on the brow of the king in one of the ceremonies of the coronation. Ramesses III mentions the ceremony in these words: "Since [the day when] I sat upon the throne of Harakhty and the Great Enchantress was fixed upon my head like Ra." Haremhab, also with reference to his coronation, says that the Great Enchantress established herself on his brow and that the ceremony took place in the Great House *(per wer)*, of which this shrine is a model.

In spite of the intimate nature of the scenes in general, at least three — the two on the back wall and the presentation of the necklace and counterpoise — depict episodes in the coronation of the king; they are, moreover, ceremonies for which there is some evidence that, in the late Eighteenth Dynasty, they were performed by the queen. It seems likely, therefore, that one of the purposes of the shrine was to commemorate the king's coronation, and through the processes of magic to renew his coronation in the afterlife.

*Cairo No. 61481; Carter No. 108.*
*Shrine: Height 19⁷⁄₈ in. (50.5 cm.), width 10⁷⁄₁₆ in. (26.5 cm.), depth 12⁹⁄₁₆ in. (32.0 cm.). Sledge: Length 18¾ in. (48.0 cm.), width 12⅛ in. (30.7 cm.).*
*Carter I, 119-20, 137, pls. XXIX, LXVIII, corselet pls. XXXVII, XXXVIII; Desroches-Noblecourt 66, pls. VII-IX, LI; Fox pl. 11; Lange and Hirmer 464, pl. XXXIII; Baker 88-9, fig. 104; K. Bosse-Griffiths 100-8.*
*Exhibitions: London No. 25; U.S.S.R. No. 5.*

golden throne found in the tomb shows the queen anointing the king with unguent from a vessel; the scene on the shrine seems to represent an action of a very similar kind.

In the lower scene the king, seated on a throne and wearing the crown of Lower Egypt, raises his left hand to receive from the queen two notched palm ribs, the hieroglyphic signs for "years." Within these signs are the symbols for jubilee festivals and also amuletic signs in groups. They are attached at the bottom to single tadpoles — the sign for "one hundred thousand" — mounted on the sign for "infinity." The inscription behind the king reads: "The Son of Ra, Lord of Crowns, Tutankh-

amun has appeared in glory on the throne of Horus like Ra."

Three objects were found in the shrine: a gilded wooden pedestal with back support, part of a corselet, and a bead necklace with a large pendant. The pedestal still has the imprint of the feet of a statuette, presumably of the king and very probably made of gold. A statuette of the queen may once have stood by its side. The fragment of the corselet was probably put in the shrine after the robbery of the tomb; other parts were found in three of the boxes and scattered about the Antechamber and elsewhere. Of greater significance is the pendant attached to the necklace (illustrated above), which is in the

At the head of each stem is a flower, the middlemost being fully open and the two sides half-open. Beneath the half-open flowers are two leaves, so represented that they appear to be floating on the surface of the water. Slight traces of oil were visible in the cups when the lamp was first examined, but there was nothing to show that it had been furnished with any holders for the wicks, which, if they were not floating, could have been three or more in number.

*Cairo No. 62112; Carter No. 174.*
*Height 10⅝ in. (27.0 cm.).*
*Carter II, 31, pl. XLVII; Desroches-*
*    Noblecourt 107, 299, pl. XXIII a;*
*    Drioton 41, pl. 119; Fox 21, pl.*
*    19; J. Černý, The Valley of the*
*    Kings, 43-54.*
*Exhibitions: None.*

## 15
## EMBLEM OF ANUBIS
## COLOR PLATE 10

One of a pair, this emblem was associated with the god Anubis. The upper part, made of wood overlaid with gesso and gilded, represents a pole terminating in a lotus bud and an inflated animal skin suspended from the pole by a copper wire tail ending in a papyrus flower. The hind legs are frequently not shown, as in this example. Some representations include a separate papyrus flower with its stem entwined around the pole. The base consists of a solid alabaster (calcite) stand in which the pole is fixed. Inscribed on the base are the name and titles of Tutankhamun "given life for ever and ever" and the epithet "Beloved of Anubis who presides over the embalming booth."

    In very remote times this fetish belonged to a god named Imiut, meaning "He who is in his wrappings," who was eventually identified with Anubis, the jackal god of embalming. An early example, found in 1914 by The Metropolitan Museum of Art near the pyramid of Sesostris I (about 1971-1928 B.C.) at El Lisht,

## 14
## TRIPLE LAMP
## COLOR PLATE 10

For purposes of lighting, the ancient Egyptians used candles and lamps, both of which were included in the equipment of Tutankhamun's tomb, together with two candlesticks and two lampstands. The candle found in one of the candlesticks is described by Carter as made of "linen twisted up and bound in a spiral by a strip of linen six centimeters [2⅜ inches] wide." It was thus in the stage of its manufacture called "dry" by the Egyptians, before it had been coated with fat to become an "anointed candle." The two lampstands belonged to the same set as the candlesticks. Carter conjectured that their lamps were gold and had been stolen by the ancient robbers.

    In its essential elements, the Egyptian oil-burning lamp remained unchanged from predynastic to Roman times. Generally it consisted of a stone or pottery vessel for the oil and a wick made of braided fibers of flax. The wick could be either floating or fixed. A fixed wick required some kind of support, which might be provided either by a pottery lid pierced with a hole through which one end of the wick would be inserted into the oil or by a hole near the top of the vessel from which the wick projected. The oil was linseed, castor, or sesame. According to the Greek historian Herodotus, who visited Egypt in about 450 B.C., the lamps he saw at Sais, in the Delta, were saucers charged with salt and oil and provided with floating wicks, the purpose of the salt being to absorb water in the oil and thus reduce the amount of smoke caused by the flame.

    This triple lamp, found in Tutankhamun's Burial Chamber, is carved from a single piece of alabaster (calcite). It depicts a lotus plant growing from the bed of a pond.

was placed in a wooden shrine. Like the emblems in Tutankhamun's tomb, it consisted of a wooden rod and an alabaster stand, but the headless animal skin was real: it was stuffed with linen and wrapped in bandages like a mummy, linen pads being placed within the bandages as packing to fill the irregularities between the skin and the rod. It is easy to see how the god acquired the name "He who is in his wrappings." The stand, which resembled a vessel, was about two-thirds full of a bluish-colored substance completely dried and considered to be some kind of ointment. Tutankhamun's emblems represent a later development, not uncommon in Egyptian tomb equipment in which a model was used in place of the object itself.

This emblem and its counterpart were placed in the northwest and southwest corners of the Burial Chamber, outside the first of the four gilded wooden shrines that protected the coffins and the mummy of the king. The position may be significant because the outermost shrine corresponded in style with the pavilion in which Egyptian kings performed some of the ceremonies of their jubilee (sed) festivals, and the emblems of Anubis are shown on the monuments in connection with that pavilion. Tutankhamun did not live long enough to celebrate a jubilee, but the provision of the proper funerary equipment would have enabled him to do so in the next world. Djoser, for whom the architect Imhotep built the famous Step Pyramid at Sakkara, included in his pyramid enclosure a separate court with stone-built model shrines, so that he could enjoy repetitions of his jubilee festival in his afterlife. Tutankhamun's arrangements were, by comparison, somewhat modest.

*The Anubis emblem (Cat. no. 15) as it was found; the oars would help the king to navigate in the next world*

*Cairo No. 61374; Carter No. 194.*
*Height 65¾ in. (167.0 cm.).*
*Carter II, 32, pls. V, VI; Desroches-*
  *Noblecourt 250; Lythgoe 150-2.*
*Exhibitions: London No. 24.*

## 16
## LION UNGUENT JAR
## COLOR PLATE 10

Amenhotpe III's best-known monument outside Egypt is the temple that he built in Nubia, between the Second and the Third Cataracts, at Soleb. Among its sculptures were two lions (now in the British Museum) carved of pink Aswan granite, both probably intended to suggest to the observer the character of the king himself. The conception of the lion as

an image of the king was not new, but the manner in which it was portrayed marked a departure from precedent. Each lion is represented in a recumbent position, its head turned sideways facing the viewer and its front paws crossed. Only the sole of the farther hind paw can be seen, placed between the body and the nearer paw. One of the lions was completed, and probably taken to Soleb, before Amenhotpe died, but the other remained unfinished for more than twenty years, until

Tutankhamun completed it and recorded his act of piety toward his deceased predecessor in an inscription on the pedestal.

In view of Tutankhamun's connection with the second Soleb lion, it is at least possible that he himself was responsible for choosing the same pose for the lion on the lid of this alabaster (calcite) unguent jar. Perhaps it also represents the same underlying conception, the image in this case being suggestive not of Amenhotpe III but Tutankhamun, whose name is written on the side of the lion's body. The most striking deviation, apart from the difference in size, is the pendent tongue of red-stained ivory, a feature that is not uncommon in representations of the lion-headed god Bes and can be seen in the two heads of the god which form the abaci of the small lotus columns beneath the lid (see No. 53). Ivory, similarly stained red, was used for the pivotal pin of the lid and for the two mushroom-shaped knobs, one on the lid and the other projecting from the brow of the head of Bes below, to which the binding string, knotted and sealed, was attached. The lion's eyes are gilded, with details in black, and the nose, eyebrows, claws, and the tip of the tail are painted dark green or black. If earrings were attached to the ears, they were probably of gold and were stolen by the ancient robbers.

Lightly incised on the exterior surface of the jar are lively scenes of animals, mostly engaged in combat. The main scene on both the front and the back sections between the columns consists of a bull being attacked by a lion; in the scene on the front a hound has joined in the attack. Two of its companions are attacking an ibex. On the back, the subsidiary features are a hound chasing a gazelle, a recumbent gazelle, and a desert hare. The dark blue background is broken in both sections by desert flora. Above and below the scenes are decorative bands, the most conspicuous element in the former being pendent lotus petals. It is evident that these naturalistic representations belong to the same genre as those on the sheath of the gold dagger (No. 20) and on the ivory veneer of the ornamented chest (No. 51), but they are artistically inferior, perhaps owing to the greater difficulty experienced in carving on a curved surface.

The jar stands on two rectangular crossbars of alabaster terminating in heads of bearded Asiatics, carved in a red stone, and in heads of Negroes with ivory earrings, carved in a black stone. They are reminiscent of the bound captives of the same kind who are sometimes represented on the pedestals of statues of kings and on footstools. The addition of such a feature to this jar gives emphasis to the royal character of the lion.

When it was opened, this jar was found to contain about one pound of organic matter which, when analyzed, appeared to be mainly animal fat with about ten percent of some resin or balsam.

*Cairo No. 62119; Carter No. 211.*
*Height 10½ in. (26.8 cm.), diameter of jar 4⁷⁄₁₆ in. (12.0 cm.).*
*Carter II, 34-5, 206-10, pls. L, LI; Desroches-Noblecourt 211, pl. XLIII; Fox pl. 22.*
*Exhibitions: None.*

## 17
## GOLD STAFF
## COLOR PLATE 12

Among the many objects from this tomb that remain unparalleled in Egyptian art are two small figures of the king, one in gold and the other in silver, the feet in each case being socketed into a plate of the same metal as the figure. Beneath the plate is a tubular shaft of silver or of gold. They were found, wrapped in fine linen and bound together, on the floor between the two outermost shrines protecting the king's coffins. Apart from their material, the two figures are almost identical in every respect. The gold figure, which is shown here, is cast solid and chased. It shows the

king wearing only the blue crown and a pleated kilt with ornamented apron suspended from a girdle. His throne name is engraved on the clasp of the girdle. The upper part of the body and the feet are bare.

Nothing in the dress of the king indicates the purpose of the object. His crown (khepresh), sometimes incorrectly called the war helmet, first appears on monuments as a royal headdress at the end of the Seventeenth Dynasty and is commonly worn by Tutankhamun's predecessors in the Eighteenth Dynasty in many different circumstances: in battle, in religious and secular ceremonies, and in private life. He is represented wearing the same kind of pleated kilt shooting ostriches from his chariot (No. 18), in some of the scenes on the small gilded shrine (No. 13), and on the gilded wooden figure (No. 35). The position of the hands, with their backs facing toward the front, is an exceptional feature in figures with a close-fitting kilt; normally this pose is found only when the kilt is of a different type with a triangular frontal projection. Perhaps this variation is but an extension of the regular practice of Egyptian sculptors, when carving in relief, of avoiding whenever possible depicting the hands in profile.

In form, this piece immediately

suggests the standards carried by priests and officials in state and religious ceremonies. As a rule, however, such standards consist of a long staff surmounted by a cult object resting on a flat base. The cult objects include birds and animals sacred to particular gods and, exceptionally, even mummiform figures, but not human figures. Furthermore, the staffs are considerably longer than those of this piece and its companion in silver. Possibly these were more in the nature of wands than standards, or conceivably marking pegs used in some ceremony. The unmistakably childlike appearance of the king might suggest that the ceremony was his coronation, which occurred when he was about nine, but why they should have been made of two different metals and how they were employed cannot be explained. Nevertheless his age and consequently his shortness of stature may account for the reduction in length of the staff.

*Cairo No. 61665; Carter No. 235a.*
*Height 51⁹⁄₁₆ in. (131.5 cm.), height of figure 3½ in. (9.0 cm.).*
*Carter II, 35, pl. VII; Desroches-Noblecourt 71, 176; Fox pl. 23; Aldred 90, pl. 150.*
*Exhibitions: U.S.A. No. 15; Paris No. 15; Japan No. 12; London No. 22; U.S.S.R. No. 20.*

# 18
## OSTRICH-FEATHER FAN
## COLOR PLATE 11

An inscription on the handle of this fan states that it is made of "ostrich feathers obtained by His Majesty when hunting in the desert east of Heliopolis." Stumps of the feathers may still be seen in the holes on the outer edge of the palm. When complete it consisted of fifteen white and fifteen brown feathers, arranged in alternate colors. The feathers had been almost entirely devoured by insects when it was found on the floor of the Burial Chamber between the innermost of the four golden shrines shielding the coffins of the king. It is made of wood covered with sheet gold.

Embossed on each face of the palm are lively scenes of the king hunting the ostriches. On the front he is shown riding in his chariot and shooting with his bow at two ostriches, one of which is already on the ground. His hound, in hot pursuit, is about to despatch the birds. The king wears a short wig with two streamers, a short leopard-skin corselet, and a kilt with ornate apron. On his left wrist is an archer's leather bracer. In order that his hands may be free to use his bow, he has put the reins around his body. The richly caparisoned horses, depicted in full gallop, have hogged manes, and ostrich plumes and sun's disks fixed to the headstalls of the bridles. An object shaped like an animal's tail and suspended near the shoulder behind the girth is found on horses of this period when decked for ceremonial occasions; its function is not clear and it may be merely decorative. The chariot is a light vehicle reminiscent of a curricle, made of wood and fitted with a sun's disk projecting above the saddle and attached to either the yoke or the front end of the pole. A bow case is strapped to the body of the chariot, inside the wheels. The quiver for the arrows is suspended from the back of the king's girdle, its handle resembling a long tail. Behind the chariot is the hieroglyphic sign for "life" *(ankh)*, with human hands and feet, carrying a fan of the same kind as this fan. The inscription above this composite figure, "May all protection of life attend him" (i.e. the king), although a common formula, is probably intended to emphasize the symbolical nature of the figure. Within the bow are two hieroglyphic signs meaning "possessor of a strong arm," a regular epithet referring to a king, but here with special application to his strength with the bow. The remainder of the field is occupied with desert flowers, perhaps thistles, and the inscription: "The good god Nebkheperura, given life for ever like Ra."

On the reverse side of the palm the king is shown returning from the hunt. The spirited horses are held in check, the reins being now in the king's hands together with his bow and a whip. He has put on a long pleated garment and what appears to be a shoulder wrap with "feathered" fringes. The form of the "feathers" does not suggest that they are ostrich plumes, as some writers have supposed. Two attendants in front of the chariot carry the two ostriches shot by the king on their shoulders. In view of the weight of these birds (about 345 lbs. fully grown if they belong to the species *Struthio Camelus* L., which existed in Egypt until some 150 years ago), it is not likely that the scene, at least in detail, is to be interpreted literally. The explanatory inscription, which fills most of the upper part of the field, reads: "The good god who secures [the quarry] in hunting, who strives [?] and engages in combat [?] in every desert [or "who campaigns and fights against every foreign land"], who shoots to kill like [the goddess] Bastet, his horses are like bulls when they convey the King of Upper and Lower Egypt, the Lord of the Two Lands, possessor of a strong arm, Nebkheperura, given life for ever like Ra." The group of hieroglyphic signs immediately behind the quiver, "given all life," is probably to be taken separately and not as part of the main inscription.

Fans of this kind were regularly carried by attendants in royal processions at court and in religious ceremonies, their modern counterparts being the flabella borne in processions in Rome behind the pope when seated on the *sedia gestatoria*. The characteristic features are the long handle terminating in a knob at the lower end and in a stylized papyrus or lotus flower at the top, a semicircular or elongated palm, and several long ostrich plumes. They were used chiefly as sunshades. Another type of fan, carried as a symbol of office, generally had a shorter handle and a single plume.

*Cairo No. 62001; Carter No. 242.*
*Length of handle 37⅜ in. (95 cm.),*
*height of palm 4⅛ in. (10.5 cm.),*
*width of palm 7¼ in. (18.5 cm.).*

*The gold fan (Cat. no. 18) and its crumbling ostrich plumes lying between the third and fourth shrines*

*Carter II, 15, 16, 46, 242, 243, pls.*
*LXI A, LXII; Desroches-*
*Noblecourt 71, 205, 298, pl. XX;*
*Fox pl. 24.*
*Exhibitions: Paris No. 25; London*
*No. 23; U.S.S.R. No. 21.*

## 19
## DOUBLE CASE
## COLOR PLATE 11

The character of the decoration of this handsome gold case, which consists of two small boxes, each in the form of a cartouche (see No. 28), seems to indicate that it was a piece of funerary equipment. Its purpose would have been difficult to determine if some of its contents – a brown substance – had not been preserved, leaving no room for doubt that it had held an unguent of some kind. Wooden unguent spoons in the New Kingdom were often carved in the shape of either a cartouche or the related *shen* sign (see No. 28), perhaps in the belief that the magic properties thought to be inherent in the symbol would impart permanence to the virtue of the unguent held in the spoons.

Set side by side and surmounted by solar disks with plumes, the two boxes are attached at the base to a low silver pedestal. Each box is provided with a lid that has a mushroom-shaped knob. Although it is not impossible that the two compartments were intended for different unguents, a more probable reason for the duality of the design would seem to be that cartouches usually occurred in pairs in inscriptions, one engraved with a king's throne name and the other with his personal name. In this piece, however, the cartouches do not enclose his names but representations of the king, two on the front and two on the back.

All four cartouches are alike in their general pattern: the central and dominant feature is the figure of Tutankhamun squatting on the *heb* sign beneath the sun's disk with uraei and pendent *ankh* signs. In both pairs the figures face inward, but, whereas those on the front are identical, those on the back represent the king with fair skin in one cartouche and, in the other, with a black head and neck. Only on the front was it necessary to fix knobs to correspond with the knobs on the lid as terminals for knotted strings with seals.

Both the front figures show the king in a long pleated robe and wearing a broad bead collar. It is noticeable that in the left-hand figure one sleeve of the robe reaches the wrist but the other sleeve stops at the elbow; in the right-hand figure the sleeves are more equal in length. The most significant feature, however, is the blue glass imitation on the side lock of plaited hair that projects from the tight-fitting cap on his head. A thousand years before the time of Tutankhamun, in the Old Kingdom, boys were frequently represented wearing the side lock, but in the New Kingdom it was usually a mark of a prince or of a certain class of priest. It was also a regular feature in the iconography of the child-god Harpocrates. In the gold shrine discussed earlier (No. 13), the young queen Ankhesenamun can be seen in a headdress with a plaited side lock; she also wears a side lock in a scene carved in ivory on the lid of the ornate chest, No. 51, but in that case the style is different. Here Tutankhamun, although his youthfulness is emphasized by the side lock, wears the uraeus on the front of the Amarna

cartouche on the back of this case (in which his arms, hands, and feet are not shown in black), is represented with black skin in two life-size wooden statues that stood outside the door leading to the Burial Chamber of his tomb. Clearly the color has no ethnic significance, but its precise meaning is not easy to explain; it may not be the same in every instance. Black was associated with regeneration, probably because it was the color of the fertile soil of Egypt – the source of plant life – and a figure so painted might benefit from the supposed regenerative properties of the color. Some figures of kings may, however, have been painted black in imitation of ebony, a material that had to be brought from Punt, called "god's land" and probably located in the region of Eritrea and Somaliland. It was highly prized, no doubt because of its color. But neither of these explanations would fully account for the partial coloring in the figure. Another peculiarity is that the *khepresh* crown (see No. 17) on his head and the pendent streamers behind are tinted with black and are in marked contrast with the bright blue crown and light streamers in the companion cartouche. In both the cartouches the king holds the crook and flail in one hand and rests the other hand on his knee.

On the outer side of each box (one illustrated at the left) is a figure of the god of eternity, Heh, kneeling on the *heb* sign and holding in each hand a long, notched palm rib, the hieroglyphic sign for "year." Over one arm is slung the sign for "life" *(ankh)*. At the base of each palm rib is a tadpole mounted on a coil of rope (see No. 10) and the meaning of the whole emblem is a wish that the years of the king may amount to "one hundred thousand times infinity." His throne name, Nebkheperura, is written with a scarab with open wings above the god's head and is repeated below together with his personal name, both in cartouches surmounted by solar disks.

The only visible decoration on

the silver pedestal is a band of "life" and "dominion" signs engraved in groups of three on the outer faces of all four sides. Concealed from view, on the underside (shown at the left) is a pleasing composition consisting of four clusters of papyrus flowers and buds and poppies, arranged in two antithetical pairs. At the foot of each cluster is a series of wavy lines representing the leaves of the papyrus. The poppy, which does not appear in Egyptian art until the New Kingdom, was not a native of the country; it was probably brought from Palestine with many other Asiatic plants during the campaigns of Tutankhamun's predecessors in the Eighteenth Dynasty. All around the clusters are pintail ducks, either in flight or alighting on the petals of the open papyrus flowers. In its general style it is very reminiscent of the paintings of marsh scenes that adorned the floors of some of the halls in Akhenaton's palace at Amarna.

The predominant material in the inlay is polychrome glass, in imitation of lapis lazuli, turquoise, and red jasper. Small pieces of these semiprecious stones may, however, have been used, interspersed with glass, in some of the decorative elements such as the *heb* signs and the necklaces. The solar disks on the front and back of the case are made of either translucent calcite or quartz with a pigment resembling the color of carnelian at the rear, and the same material has been applied to the exposed parts of the king's body and also to the tails of the streamers. With the exception of the plumes on the lid, which are made of cloisonné work, nearly all the ornamention is highly embossed and chased.

*Carter No. 61496; Carter No. 240* bis.
*Height 6⅝₁₆ in. (16.0 cm.), width 3⅞₁₆ in. (8.8 cm.), depth 1¹¹⁄₁₆ in. (4.3 cm.).*
*Carter II, 90, 255, pl. LXXIV;*
*Desroches-Noblecourt 69, 297, pl. XIII.*
*Exhibitions: None.*

type of cap with streamers and in his hands he holds the crook and flail (see No. 5), all of which indicate that he had already been crowned, an event that probably took place when he was about nine years of age.

Certain gods, notably Osiris, Amun, and Min, are sometimes depicted with black skin. There are also several paintings and statues of kings of both the Middle and the New Kingdoms, and a number of paintings of Queen Ahmose Nafretari, mother of Amenhotpe I, in which the color of her skin is black. Tutankhamun, in addition to the figure in the left-hand

# 20
## GOLD DAGGER AND SHEATH
## COLOR PLATE 14

Daggers were used by the ancient Egyptians from predynastic times onward, though examples dating from the Old Kingdom (about 2700-2180 B.C.) are exceedingly rare. During the Middle Kingdom (about 2100-1700 B.C.) and the New Kingdom (about 1570-1000 B.C.) they were generally made of copper or bronze; gold, apart from its use for purposes of embellishment, was probably reserved for royalty. Queen Ahhotpe, mother of Ahmose I, the founder of the Eighteenth Dynasty, had, in her funerary equipment, a solid gold dagger and sheath, both of which are now in the Cairo Museum. Tutankhamun's mummy was provided with two daggers encased in gold sheaths, one with an iron blade and the other with a blade of hardened gold. The latter specimen is shown here.

As an illustration of the goldsmith's artistic ability and technical skill, this dagger, and particularly its sheath, are among the outstanding pieces of the collection. On the top of the pommel (illustrated in the drawing) are the king's cartouches in applied embossed gold and a wreath of lily palmettes in cloisonné work. On the underside are two figures of falcons holding in each talon the hieroglyphic symbol for "infinity" (shen). The falcon was often represented in Egyptian art holding this symbol and, with wings outstretched, protecting a king (see No. 6): it was probably intended to serve an amuletic purpose in this instance also. A similar motif appears on the haft of a dagger in the Metropolitan Museum bearing the same name of Thutmose I (about 1524-1518 B.C.) and it may have been a characteristic feature of royal daggers at this period. Below the pommel, the haft is decorated with alternate bands of geometric designs in very fine granulated goldwork and lily-palmette designs in gold cloisonné work of semiprecious stones

and glass, a central band of minute red and blue circular disks breaking the regularity of the palmette ornamentation. At the base of the hilt, applied in gold wire, is a band of continuous spirals within a rope-pattern border, thus conveying to the eye the suggestion that the haft is bound to the blade.

In striking contrast with the ornate haft, the decoration of the blade, which is tinged with red, is simple. Incised at the top on both faces is a plain horizontal band, which also suggests a tie, over a design consisting of a diamond-pattern chain bordered beneath by two horizontal lines, the spaces between the diamonds being filled with dots. Under this frieze is engraved an elegant palmette with poppies surmounting two perpendicular grooves that converge at the base and resemble floral stems.

The front of the gold sheath is almost entirely covered with a feather pattern in cloisonné work, relieved at the top by a palmette frieze and at the pointed base by a jackal's head. Of far greater interest is the elaborate design on the reverse. First comes a line of inscription reading: "The good god, possessor of a strong arm, Nebkheperura, given life." A row of continuous spirals follows and then two loops of palmette design, by means of which the sheath was attached to the girdle. The main scene, embossed in high relief, is composed of the following elements: an ibex attacked by a lion, a calf with a hound on its back biting the calf's tail, a leopard and a lion attacking a male ibex from above and below, a hound biting a bull, and lastly a calf in full flight. Interspersed between the animals are stylized plants, while a more elaborate floral device occupies the pointed base.

Although there is no reason to doubt that this sheath was made in Egypt, the decoration of the reverse includes artistic features that have a foreign appearance. The band of continuous spirals, the style of the rosette on the shoulder of the second

lion (see Nos. 16, 48), the summary treatment of the skins of the animals, and the floral motif at the base have parallels in the art of northern Syria at this period and they also have Minoan or Mycenaean affinities. Scenes of workshops painted on the walls of private tombs at Thebes sometimes include Asiatic craftsmen at work side by side with the far more numerous Egyptian artisans; they were very probably employed on account of their ability to reproduce artistic styles that were familiar to them but new to the Egyptians. Like so many other importations in the history of Egypt, however, these innovations were quickly absorbed and given the general character of native products.

*Cairo No. 61584; Carter No. 256dd.*
*Dagger: Length 12½ in. (31.9 cm.), blade 7¾ in. (20.1 cm.).*
*Sheath: Length 8¼ in. (21.0 cm.), width 1¹¹⁄₁₆ (4.4 cm.).*
*Carter II, 16, 131-2, pls. LXXXVII A, LXXXVIII A,B; Desroches-Noblecourt 232-3, pl. XXI a, b; Fox pl. 37; Drioton 42, pl. 132; Gardiner frontispiece; Schaeffer 33-4.*
*Exhibitions: U.S.A. No. 1; Paris No. 19; Japan No. 1; London No. 36; U.S.S.R. No. 25.*

## 21
## FLEXIBLE BEAD BRACELET
## COLOR PLATE 15

Thirteen bracelets, illustrated in the photograph at the right, were placed on the forearms of Tutankhamun's mummy, seven on the right and six on the left. Apart from these thirteen, there were other bracelets among the mummy wrappings and elsewhere in the tomb. This bracelet was placed on the right forearm, near the elbow. Its wristband is composed of nine rows of gold, faience, and glass beads threaded between six gold spacer bars that resemble the gold beads and

keep the nine rows in position. The clasp, which is like a pegged mortise and tenon joint, consists of three members: a hollow bar with a central slot (the bar itself being attached to one end of a gold cloison inlaid with a carnelian *udjat* eye), a tenon which projects from the terminal at the free end of the wristband and fits into the slot, and a removable gold pin to hold the tenon in the slot. On the back of the cloison there is the inscription "Lord of the Two Lands, image of Ra, Nebkheperura, ruler of what is in order, given life like Ra for ever and ever." The engraver has inverted the signs for the Two Lands. It is exceptional, but not without parallel, to find the epithet "ruler of what is in order" (see No. 22) after the king's throne name. Both the eye and the cloison have a figure of an uraeus with the double crown at the end opposite to the clasp.

The *udjat* eye consists of a human eye and eyebrow to which are added the markings on a falcon's head; it is thus symbolical of both Horus, son of Osiris and Isis, who is represented in human form, and the sky god named Horus, who is represented either as a falcon or as a man with a falcon's head. The word *udjat* means "sound, healthy" and it was used by the ancient Egyptians as a name for the eye which Horus had lost when fighting with the god Seth to avenge the murder of Osiris. According to the myth, Seth tore the eye into fragments, but Thoth, the god of writing, wisdom, and magic, found the fragments and put them together. He restored the eye to health by spitting on it and then gave it back to Horus, and he, in turn, gave it to the dead Osiris to eat, thereby bringing him back to life.

Filial piety was one of the virtues symbolized by the *udjat* eye: it could serve as a substitute for any of the offerings that an eldest son was supposed to provide daily at the tomb of his father. It was also thought to be a potent amulet against sickness and to be capable of restor-

ing the dead to life, as it had done for Osiris. Both the right eye and the left eye are represented in the *udjat* form, but the right is more common, perhaps through the influence of another myth, according to which the sun and the moon were the right and left eyes of the sky god and the sun was regarded as the more powerful. With the exception of the scarab, the *udjat* was the most popular amulet in ancient Egypt.

*Cairo No. 62372; Carter No. 256 oo. Length 6⅜ in. (16.2 cm.), width 1¹⁄₁₆ in. (2.7 cm.).*
*Carter II, 129, 267, pls. XXXIII, LXXXVI A (2nd from top); Desroches-Noblecourt 231, fig. 142; Aldred, Jewels, 226, pl. 112; Wilkinson 106.*
*Exhibitions: None.*

## 22
## GOLD RINGS
## COLOR PLATE 15

Five of the finest gold rings found in Tutankhamun's tomb are shown in Color Plate 15. Depicted on the massive ring in the foreground is the falcon-headed god Ra-Harakhty, whose name means Ra Horus of the Horizon. Since remote antiquity the cult of the sun god Ra had been centered at Heliopolis, near Cairo. Horus was the god personified by the Upper Egyptian kings who conquered Lower Egypt, where Heliopolis was situated, at the beginning of the historical period. For political reasons, the cults of the two gods were unified, and the composite god Ra-Harakhty came into being. In the Eighteenth Dynasty the capital was established at Thebes, 400 miles to the south, and Amun was recognized as the state god. Probably to restore some of Ra-Harakhty's lost prestige and to counteract the power of the priests of Amun, Tutankhamun's predecessors Amenhotpe III and his son Amenhotpe IV built sanctuaries at Karnak to Ra-Harakhty. Amenhotpe

IV later moved the capital north to Amarna, adopted the name Akhenaton, and suppressed the cults of all the gods except that of the sun's disk, Aton. Tutankhamun's accession to the throne, followed by his revival of the old cults, restored Ra-Harakhty to the position he had occupied in Egypt before Akhenaton.

The next ring bears Tutankhamun's original personal name, Tutankhaton, and his throne name, Nebkheperura. The change to Tutankhamun was made when he was about nine, when he was crowned by the priests of Amen-Ra at Karnak. The king thus detached himself from the cult of Aton and declared his adherence to the older cult of Amun.

Next is shown a heavy ring depicting Amun, or Amen-Ra as he is called in the inscription. When Amun became the official state god during the Eighteenth Dynasty the important sun god of Heliopolis became associated with him at Thebes under the name Amen-Ra. His cult was the most powerful of those that Akhenaton suppressed.

Second from the top is one of the two rings found on the king's mummy; it depicts Tutankhamun holding an image of the goddess Maat. Maat personified the action of the creator of the universe, Atum, when he established the right order in nature and society. The ring illustrates a ceremony performed every morning at the temple of Karnak: after opening the door of the shrine containing a statue of Amun, the king or the high priest knelt and offered it an image of Maat.

The ring at the top of the color plate is another representation of Ra-Harakhty, to whom the king presents an offering.

*In ascending order: Carter Nos. 256 vv, 256 vv, 44 f, 256 ccc, 44 h.*
*Carter I, 114, 138, pl. XXX, LXVII A; II, 127, 130, pl. LXXXV; Desroches-Noblecourt 231-2, pl. 143; Aldred, Jewels, 217, pl. 91; Wilkinson 130-4.*

## 23
## VULTURE COLLAR
## COLOR PLATE 13

This flexible gold collar, in the form of the vulture of the goddess Nekhbet (see No. 24), was laid on the thorax of the king's mummy so that it covered the whole of the chest and extended upward to the shoulders. Collars and necklaces were placed on Egyptian mummies not as objects of adornment but to provide magical protection. They were also represented on the cartonnage covers of mummies and on the lids of anthropoid coffins. Among the many collar amulets painted on the walls of rectangular wooden coffins dating from the Middle Kingdom are four made of gold and inlaid on the outer surface, shaped to represent a falcon, a vulture, a winged cobra, and a combined vulture and cobra.

Tutankhamun's mummy, which was more than half a millennium later in date than these coffins, was equipped with all these inlaid collars except the cobra collar, and also with all four collars in sheet gold without inlay. They were purely funerary in character and very different from the bead or gold collars worn in life.

The elongated wings, set in a circular fashion, are divided into "districts." They are composed of two hundred and fifty segments, engraved on the back and inlaid on the front with "feathers" of polychrome glass in imitation of turquoise, jasper, and lapis lazuli. The segments were held together by thread that passed through small golden eyelets projecting from the upper and lower edges. On one side margin of each segment, except in the district known as the lesser coverts, there is a border of minute

gold beads to divide its feathers from those of its neighbor. The body of the bird is inlaid in the same manner as the lesser coverts, while the tail feathers resemble the primary and the secondary districts of the wings. Both the beak and the eye in the delicately chased head are made of obsidian. In each of the talons the bird grasps the hieroglyphic sign for "infinity" *(shen)*, inlaid with red and blue glass. A floral-shaped counterpoise *(mankhet)*, which was attached by gold wires to eyelets at the back of the wings, hung down the back of the mummy.

*Cairo No. 61876; Carter*
*No. 256 mmm.*
*Height 15⁹⁄₁₆ in. (39.5 cm.),*
*width 18¾ in. (48 cm.).*
*Carter II, 123-4, pl. LXXX B;*
*M. Vilímková pl. 45; Wilkinson*
*XXVI, pl. XXXVI A; Aldred,*

Jewels, 225-6, pl. III.
Exhibitions: Paris No. 20; London
No. 40; U.S.S.R. No. 34.

# 24
# NECKLACE
# WITH VULTURE PENDANT
# COLOR PLATE 14

Tutankhamun's mummy was bandaged in layers, the appropriate amulets and jewelry being placed in each layer, and the innermost layers contained his personal possessions. This necklace was suspended from his neck in the eleventh or twelfth layer, close to the mummy, and therefore very probably it was a piece that he had worn during his lifetime. The pendant consists of a representation of the vulture goddess of Upper Egypt, Nekhbet, with the outer ends of the wings folded downward resembling a cloak. It is made of solid gold, encrusted on the front with blue glass, apart from the lesser coverts of the wings, which are encrusted with red glass edged with green, and the tips of the tail feathers, which are also encrusted with red glass. In its talons it holds the hieroglyphic sign for "infinity" (shen), inlaid with carnelian and blue glass. The gold head, turned sideways, and the neck are delicately rendered in a most realistic manner, the effect being heightened by the wrinkled occiput, the obsidian eyes, and the lapis lazuli beak. On the chased reverse the vulture is shown wearing a miniature necklace and pendant, modeled in high relief: the pendant is composed of Tutankhamun's cartouche surmounted by the sun's disk and ostrich plumes, flanked by two uraei. Fastenings for the suspensory chains are attached to the upper edges of the wings. The chains are formed of rectangular links of gold and lapis lazuli inlaid, on the front, with concentric circles of colored glass and bordered on the outer sides with minute gold and glass beads; some of the lapis lazuli links had decayed before the necklace was found. The clasp consists of two falcons with heads turned backward and resting on their scapulae. Made of gold encrusted with lapis lazuli, feldspar, onyx, carnelian, and green glass, they are connected by a gold tenon on the inner side of the bird, which slides into a gold mortise on the inner side of the other bird.

Nekhbet, whose name means "She who belongs to Nekheb," was originally simply the local goddess of Nekheb, the modern Elkab on the east bank of the Nile, about halfway between Luxor and Aswan. She owed her importance in dynastic times to her previous adoption by the predynastic kings of Upper Egypt, whose seat lay at Nekhen (Hieraconpolis), across the river from Nekheb. According to tradition, the last of these kings, Menes, completed the conquest of Lower Egypt, the patron deity of whose kings was the cobra goddess Wadjet, and united the two kingdoms under his sovereignty. The vulture and the cobra thus became the symbols of this unification and also the tutelary deities of the kings. Their heads were often placed side by side on the front of the headdresses worn by kings on state occasions, and on the headdresses of their statues and other representations. Frequently the entire cobra was reproduced in this setting, and they were also depicted singly, as the vulture in this pendant. It is said that this species of vulture (Gyps fulvus) now has its habitat in Middle and Upper Egypt and further south, but is seldom seen in Lower Egypt.

Cairo No. 61892; Carter No. 256ppp.
Pendant: Maximum height 2⁹/₁₆ in.
     (6.5 cm.), maximum width
     4⁵/₁₆ in. (11.0 cm.).
Carter II, 124, pl. LXXXIV;
     Desroches-Noblecourt 229-31, pl.
     XXXVII a; Drioton 42, pl. 131;
     Fox pl. 36; Lange and Hirmer pl.
     XLI; Nims fig. 31; Vilímková
     32-3; Aldred, Jewels, 128-9, 221,
     pl. 103; Wilkinson 140-1, pl. LIV.
Exhibitions: Paris No. 18; London
     No. 43; U.S.S.R. No. 28.

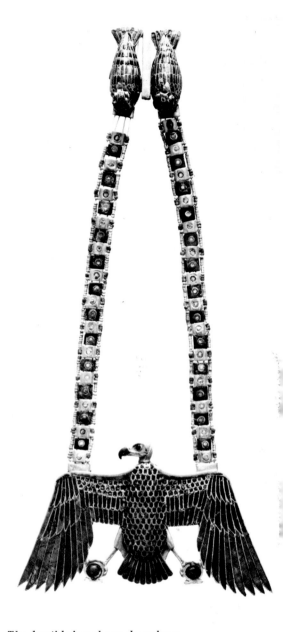

The detail below shows the vulture wearing the miniature pectoral with Tutankhamun's cartouche (Cat. no. 24)

# THE GOLD MASK
## COLOR PLATE 12

This mask of solid gold, beaten and burnished, was placed over the head and shoulders of Tutankhamun's mummy, outside the linen bandages in which the whole body was wrapped. Although it is difficult to judge how closely the face represents a true likeness of the king, it is at least an approximation. The rather narrow eyes, the shape of the nose, the fleshy lips, and the cast of the chin are all in agreement with the features visible in his mummy, and the whole countenance is unmistakably youthful. Perhaps it is slightly idealized, but essentially it seems to be a faithful portrait.

Mummification and the various rites connected with it had a double purpose: the preservation of the body to receive the soul, and the creation of a likeness of the god Osiris. Through the action of imitative magic a dead body, mummified and bandaged so that outwardly it resembled the form of Osiris, would, so the Egyptians believed, be reanimated in the same way as the body of the god had been revivified after death, thereby enabling him to become ruler of the kingdom of the dead. Tutankhamun's body was mummified and bandaged in the prescribed Osirian fashion, and a crook and flail, the emblems of Osiris (see No. 5), were placed in artificial hands of burnished gold outside the bandages over his chest. A hieroglyphic inscription on a strip of gold beneath the hands puts the following words in the mouth of the sky goddess Nut: "Osiris, King of Upper and Lower Egypt and Lord of the Two Lands Nebkheperura, your soul lives and your veins are healthy." It is clear therefore that the dead king was regarded as an Osiris. But the Osirian creed never superseded completely the solar cult of the Pyramid Age, according to which deceased kings were thought to become identified with the sun god Ra, whose body was made of gold and his hair of lapis lazuli. Tutankhamun's mask with its gold face and neck, and its eyebrows and eyelashes of lapis lazuli, perhaps preserves a relic of this belief. The hands, which are the only other physical members represented, being also of gold, help to create the illusion that the whole body was made of this metal, an illusion heightened by the darkening effect of the unguents that had been applied to all the linen bandages.

The stripes of the *nemes* headdress are made of blue glass in imitation of lapis lazuli, and the same material has been used for the inlay of the plaited false beard. The vulture's head upon the brow, symbolizing sovereignty over Upper Egypt, is also made of solid gold, apart from the beak, which is made of horn-colored glass, and the inlay of the eyes, which is missing. By its side is the cobra, symbolizing sovereignty over Lower Egypt, its body made of solid gold, its head of dark blue faience, its eyes of gold cloisonné inlaid with translucent quartz backed with a red pigment, and its hood inlaid with carnelian, lapis lazuli, turquoise-colored glass, and quartz. The eyebrows, eyelids, and kohl marks extending sideways from the eyes are made of lapis lazuli and the eyes of quartz and obsidian. Caruncles (small red patches) are shown on the inner and outer canthi of the eyes — a frequent mistake in Egyptian reproductions of the human eye, which in nature shows a caruncle on the inner canthus only. The lobes of the ears are pierced for earrings, but when the mask was found the holes were covered with disks of gold foil. A triple-string necklace of gold and faience disk beads has also been removed from the mask in order to reveal the neck. On the chest, extending from shoulder to shoulder, is a broad collar encrusted with segments of lapis lazuli, quartz, and green feldspar with a lotus-bud border of colored-glass cloisonné work. At each end of the collar is a terminal in the form of a falcon's head of gold encrusted with obsidian and colored glass.

The inscription engraved on the shoulders and on the back of the mask is a spell that first appears on masks of the Middle Kingdom, some five hundred years before the time of Tutankhamun. It was later incorporated in the Book of the Dead (Chapter 151 B). Intended for the protection of the mask, it identifies its various parts with the corresponding physical members of different gods, addressing them individually: "... Your right eye is the night bark [of the sun god], your left eye is the day bark, your eyebrows are [those of] the Ennead of the Gods, your forehead is [that of] Anubis, the nape of your neck is [that of] Horus, your locks of hair are [those of] Ptah-Soker. [You are] in front of the Osiris [Tutankhamun], he sees thanks to you, you guide him to the goodly ways, you smite for him the confederates of Seth so that he may overthrow your enemies before the Ennead of the Gods in the great Castle of the Prince, which is in Heliopolis ... the Osiris, the king of Upper Egypt Nebkheperura, deceased, given life like Ra."

*Cairo No. 60672; Carter No. 256 A.*
*Height 21¼ in. (54.0 cm.), width 15⅞₆ in. (39.3 cm.).*
*Carter II, 83, 85, 88, frontispiece, pls. XXV, LXXIII; Desroches-Noblecourt 74, 236, 300, fig. 73, pl. XXVI; Aldred, Art, 92, pl. 156; Drioton 42, pl. 134; Fox 24, pls. 32-3, Lange and Hirmer pl. XXXVIII; Piankoff, pl. 17.*
*Exhibitions: Paris No. 43; Japan No. 45; London No. 50; U.S.S.R. No. 17.*

*Tutankhamun's gold mask as it was found (Cat. no. 25)*

## 26
## PECTORAL WITH SOLAR AND LUNAR EMBLEMS
## COLOR PLATE 16

Composite forms of two related symbols were common in religious iconography as a way of indicating two originally separate conceptions that had been fused in the course of time, and such a fusion is dramatically illustrated by the central motif of this gold cloisonné pectoral. In Egyptian symbolism the sun god could be represented both as a scarab (see No. 32) and as a falcon (see No. 27): here he is symbolized by a scarab of translucent greenish-yellow chalcedony that serves as the body of a falcon with wings outstretched. It has the forelegs of a scarab and, at the back, falcon's legs of gold. In both talons it grasps the hieroglyphic sign for "infinity" (shen) and in one an open lily, while the other holds a lotus flower and buds. Bordering this motif on each side is a cobra with the sun's disk

on its head and a long tail extending upward to form an outer frame for the tops of the falcon wings. A band of blue and red disks stretches from one cobra to the other beneath the winged scarab.

The designer of this pectoral, having produced a twofold symbol of the sun, repeated the technique, but less effectively, in the case of the moon. Above the winged scarab, supported by its front legs and the tips of its wings, is a gold bark, its hull inlaid in the center with turquoise. That it is the bark of the moon is shown by the left "Eye of Horus" which was one of the symbols of the moon, the right "Eye of Horus" being a symbol of the sun. Two cobras with sun's disks flank the eye, perhaps as symbols of Upper and Lower Egypt, on both of which the moon shines. The eye alone would have been enough to indicate that the bark belonged to the moon, but the artist has added to it the disk and crescent of the moon. The disk is appropriately made of silver and

applied to its surface are small golden figures of the ibis-headed moon god Thoth, the king, and Ra-Harakhty, the two former wearing the moon's disk and crescent and Ra-Harakhty the sun's disk with uraeus.

As a kind of fringe at the base of the pectoral are blue lotus flowers, complex buds, and papyrus flowers projecting from poppy buds, all separated at the point where the stem joins the flower or the bud by roundels of concentric circles.

This pectoral is inlaid with carnelian, lapis lazuli, calcite, obsidian (?), turquoise, and red, blue, green, black, and white glass.

*Cairo No. 61884; Carter No. 267 d.*
*Height 5⅞ in. (14.9 cm.), width 5¹¹⁄₁₆ in. (14.5 cm.).*
*Carter III, 76, pl. XIX B; Desroches-Noblecourt pl. XXXVI; Wilkinson XXX, pl. L; Aldred, Jewels, 223, pl. 106; Vilímková pl. 36.*
*Exhibitions: London No. 30; U.S.S.R. No. 35.*

*This falcon pectoral (Cat. no. 27) is buried upside-down in the lower right corner*

## 27
## FALCON PECTORAL
## COLOR PLATE 16

A problem that must have perplexed the Egyptians in remote antiquity was how the sun traveled across the sky each day. In prehistoric times the sun cult had been adopted by a number of the scattered communities that had settled along the banks of the Nile, and different ideas had evolved to account for the daily phenomenon. After the unification of the country under one ruler – an event that marked both the beginning of the historical period and the foundation of the First Dynasty in about 3100 B.C. – the ideas conceived by the priests of the solar cult at Heliopolis began to gain wider recognition and, not many centuries later, the Heliopolitan creed became the state religion. In reaching that position it had not required the suppression of other cults, but it had absorbed some of

their beliefs and conceptions and, in particular, some of the ideas developed by other solar cults. These extraneous ideas were not allowed to supersede or supplant those that already existed in their creed; they merely supplemented them even though they were sometimes difficult to reconcile with them. Such was the case with their ideas about the passage of the sun across the sky.

According to one school of thought, the sun god, when he emerged each morning from the underworld, entered his bark "of millions of years" and, accompanied by his divine retinue, ferried across the sky until he reached the western horizon and re-entered the underworld (see No. 36). A more picturesque explanation of the daily crossing represented the power that propelled the sun as a large scarab beetle, the concept having been suggested by the common spectacle of the scarab pushing its ball of dung

along the ground (see No. 32). Yet another explanation arose from the fact that, apart from the celestial bodies, the only creatures that could support themselves in the air were those provided with wings, and in particular birds. A sun god who was worshiped in many localities was called Horus, a name that means "lofty." From very early times he was thought to be a falcon, probably because of its habit of flying high in the air. When he was identified with Ra, the sun god of Heliopolis, he became a composite god named Ra-Harakhty but retained his falcon form. It is in that form that the sun god is represented on this pectoral. The materials used in the inlay are lapis lazuli, turquoise, carnelian, and light blue glass, with perhaps obsidian for the eye. On the underside, which has four rings for suspension chains, the details of the bird are chased in the surface of the gold. In each talon it holds the signs for "life" and "infinity."

*Cairo No. 61893; Carter*
  *No. 267 m(1).*
*Width 4¹⁵⁄₁₆ in. (12.6 cm.).*
*Carter III, 66-7; Wilkinson 139, pl.*
  *LVI A; Aldred, Jewels, 222, pl.*
  *104; Vilímková 50.*
*Exhibitions: None.*

## 28
## CARTOUCHE-SHAPED BOX
## COLOR PLATE 17

Cartouche, a French word meaning an ornamental tablet for an inscription, is the name that was given by early scholars to the oval rings in which a king's throne name and personal name and the names of other members of the royal family were usually written. The personal name of the king might be followed by an epithet, which would also be included in the cartouche. A cartouche actually represents a length of rope formed into a loop by tying the two ends together. The ancient Egyptians called the cartouche *shenu*, a noun derived from a verb meaning "to encircle," the underlying idea being to represent the king as ruler of all that the sun encircled. Many of the objects illustrated in this book — the knobs of this box among them — bear a circular form of the cartouche (usually but not invariably without an inscription) the sense of which is "infinity" or "universality."

The decipherment of Egyptian hieroglyphics in the early years of the last century was greatly helped by the fact that the hieroglyphic inscription on the Rosetta Stone contained six cartouches, spaced at irregular intervals apart and all enclosing the same hieroglyphic signs written in the same order. A study of the Greek text carved beneath the hieroglyphic inscription showed that the name Ptolemy occurred at about the same distances apart as the cartouches in the hieroglyphic inscription and, if the conjecture that one text was a translation of the other was correct, it was reasonable to deduce that the hieroglyphic signs within the car-touches also spelt Ptolemy. Both the conjecture and the deduction proved to be right, and the first step toward reading the long-forgotten script of the ancient Egyptian language was thus achieved, largely through the chance discovery of a bilingual document that included a royal name written in a cartouche.

On the top of the lid of this box, rising slightly above the gilded background, are applied ebony and painted ivory hieroglyphs that render the king's personal name and his usual epithet: "Amun," "Tut," "ankh" and "ruler," "of On," "of Upper Egypt." The name of the god Amun was written first for honorific reasons, but it was read after "Tut" and "ankh." Like other Egyptian names Tutankhamun has a meaning, although it is uncertain whether it should be translated "Perfect is the life of Amun" or "Living image of Amun." On, better known by its Greek name Heliopolis, was the ancient center of the cult of the sun god Ra that is mentioned in the Old Testament. When Amun, the god of Thebes, was identified with the sun god, "On of Upper Egypt" was adopted as a name for Thebes.

On the rectangular panel, which represents the downward extension of the tied ends of the rope, are incised the king's personal name, his throne name (both in cartouches), and his Horus name, each with its appropriate title. Beneath the cartouches are written the words "Given life like Ra for ever." The ebony knobs on the lid and on the panel bear images of Heh, the god of eternity, kneeling on the hieroglyphic sign that signifies "gold" and holding in each hand a palm rib, the hieroglyph for "year." Attached to the base of each palm rib are a tadpole and the *shen* sign to convey the sense of an infinite number of hundreds of thousands of years; the sign for "life" is looped over the right arm at the elbow (see No. 2). On the god's head is the sun's disk.

Although the reddish-brown

wood has not been scientifically identified, it is believed to be of a coniferous kind. All the edges of the box and the cartouche on the lid are veneered with strips of ebony. The bands of inscription, which give the king's names and titles and some of his many epithets, are inlaid with a golden pigment on the lid and with blue frit on the box.

Most of the contents of this box, like the chests in its vicinity, had been plundered by the ancient robbers and other things had been hastily substituted by the necropolis staff (see Nos. 30-32). Included, however, were some scepters that Carter considered to be part of the original equipment, and if so the box was probably used on ceremonial occasions, possibly even at the king's coronation, when changes in regalia were required.

*Cairo No. 61490; Carter No. 269.*
*Length 25 in. (63.5 cm.), width 11⅞*

in. (30.2 cm.), height 12⅝ in.
(32.1 cm.).
Carter III, 67, pls. IV, XVI; Desroches-Noblecourt 84, 86, pls.
44-5; Aldred, Jewels, 244-5,
pls. 155-6.
Exhibitions: None.

## 29
## EARRINGS
## COLOR PLATE 17

The cartouche-shaped wooden box, No. 28, contained, among other pieces of jewelry, this remarkable pair of gold earrings. At least for royalty, earrings were a relatively recent innovation at the time of Tutankhamun. Their popularity in the New Kingdom was probably a legacy of the Hyksos invaders who brought them from Western Asia, where they had been in vogue for many centuries. Apart from a very small number which have been ascribed to the Middle Kingdom, the earliest recorded examples in Egypt were found by Sir Flinders Petrie in a tomb at Thebes that he dated to the end of the Seventeenth Dynasty (about 1580 B.C.).
At first they seem to have been worn chiefly by women, not merely by members of the nobility but also by some of those who served the nobility, such as musicians and dancers. According to one of the Amarna letters, earrings were among the principal items of jewelry brought by a Mitannian princess to Egypt at the time of her marriage to Amenhotpe III (about 1386-1349 B.C.). How soon, and to what extent, the custom was adopted by men is uncertain, but the first king whose mummy shows pierced lobes of the ears is Thutmose IV (about 1419-1386 B.C.), who lived about eighty-five years before Tutankhamun. Perhaps it is no more than a coincidence that he was the first Egyptian king to marry a Mitannian princess, because instances of men wearing earrings

occur in the wall paintings of at least two Theban tombs antedating his reign. Compared, however, with the countless representations of female wearers of earrings, the number of representations of male wearers is very small and, in the main, confined to young princes. The lobes of the ears of the mummies of several kings, including Sethy I (about 1291-1279 B.C.) and Ramesses II (about 1279-1212 B.C.), were pierced and it must be supposed that at some stage in their lives they wore earrings. Moreover, sculptures of kings from Amenhotpe III to Ramesses II often show pierced lobes. A possible explanation is that earrings were normally – though not invariably, and particularly not in Amarna times – discarded by boys when they reached manhood. Such an explanation would accord with the fact that, in spite of the profusion of other kinds of jewelry, no earrings were placed on the mummy of Tutankhamun. It would also account for the covering with gold foil of the perforations in the ears of the gold mask (see No. 25). That these earrings were actually used by Tutankhamun is highly probable, because they show signs of the kind of friction that would come from being worn.

In order to attach them to the pierced lobes of the ears, a stud-like clasp was made in two pieces, so that it could be taken apart. Each piece is composed of a short cylindrical tube closed at one end by a gold disk with raised rim, on which is mounted

a hemispherical button of transparent glass. When the clasp is closed, one tube fits inside the other. A portrait of the king appears behind one button on each earring, and is visible through the glass covering; microscopic examination suggests it is not, however, a true painting: it seems to consist of particles of colored glass fused on the under surface of the clear glass button. Two pendent uraei attached to the disks flank the portraits. Suspended on ring eyelets from the clasps are figures of hybrid birds with gold cloisonné bodies and wings of falcons and heads of ducks. The wings are curved inward so that they meet at the top to form a complete circle. In their claws the birds hold the hieroglyphic sign for "infinity" (shen). The heads are made of translucent blue glass and the bodies and wings are inlaid with quartz, calcite, colored faience, and blue, red, white, and green glass. Pendent extensions from the tails of the birds consist of openwork gold frames encrusted with alternate rows of gold and blue inlay, arranged in a feather pattern, and cylindrical blue and gold beads that terminate in five heads and hoods of uraei.

Cairo No. 61969; Carter
No. 269 a(1).
Length 4¼ in. (10.9 cm.), width
2¹/₁₆ in. (5.2 cm.).
Carter III, 74-5, pl. XVIII; Fox 28,
pl. 49; Drioton 42, pl. 130;
Riesterer pl. 40; Möller 38-45;
Wilkinson XXVII, XLV B;
Bimson 294.
Exhibitions: Paris No. 16; London
No. 39; U.S.S.R. No. 27.

## 30
## MIRROR CASE
## COLOR PLATE 18

In the Egyptian language a hand mirror was generally called "that which sees the face" (maw her), but it was also known by another word, ankh, spelt like the word meaning "life." The artist who designed this mirror case in the form of the hieroglyphic sign for "life" was no doubt deliberately indulging in a play on words. What the *ankh* sign represents is not known with certainty; the explanation accepted by most authorities is that it reproduces in a developed form the strings or straps of a sandal. In Christian times the symbol was retained as a variant for the cross, the so-called cross with a handle *(crux ansata)*.

Hand mirrors were usually kept in wooden cases, but not of this shape. As a rule the case protected only the disk of the mirror; the handle, which was often ornamented, remained exposed. Tutankhamun's case is unique. It consists of two pieces, a lid and a box, both carved in wood and covered externally with thin sheet gold. The lid was fastened to the box by means of catches at the base and silver knobs at the top to serve as terminals for a knotted and sealed cord. Inside, the box is lined with thin sheet silver. Within the loop of the *ankh* is an inlaid motif consisting of an open blue lotus flower and two buds supporting the king's throne name flanked by uraei with "infinity" *(shen)* signs and sun's disks, the inlay being colored glass with the exception of the disks, which are carnelian, and the base of the hoods of the uraei, which are quartz. The motif is probably intended to suggest to the eye the emergence of the sun god from the lotus at the time of the creation of the universe (see No. 1). Embossed upon the sheet gold of the outer surface are the king's throne name and his personal name, with their appropriate titles, repeated several times, and the standard epithets concerning his connection with the gods.

In order to fit this case the disk of the mirror must have been pearshaped, a shape that came into vogue in the Eighteenth Dynasty. It was made of polished metal, perhaps silver, as Carter conjectured, and doubtless stolen by the ancient rob-

bers. Generally, Egyptian mirrors were made of copper or bronze and were slightly elliptical in shape. A tang at the base of the disk fitted into the handle, which could be made of many different materials, including wood, ivory, ebony, stone, and metal. In earlier times mirrors, which were owned by both men and women, were a mark of social distinction. A sage, writing about the chaotic conditions that prevailed in Egypt probably between the Old and Middle Kingdoms (about 2100 B.C.), described the reduced status of the upper classes and the corresponding elevation of that of the lower classes in these words: "She who had [formerly] to look at her face in water is now the owner of a mirror [*ankh*]."

Tutankhamun's mirror and case may have been personal possessions, which he used in his lifetime, but it seems more likely that they were specially made for his tomb equipment. In the Middle Kingdom (about

2000 B.C.) mirrors were regularly included among the objects painted on the wooden coffins and intended to assume reality for use in the next world. Sometimes they were actually placed under the head of a mummy inside the linen wrappings. In the case of an Eleventh Dynasty official named Wah, whose tomb at Thebes was excavated by the Metropolitan Museum in the season 1919-1920, the mirror was found in front of his face—a reminder of its name "that which sees the face."

This piece was among the objects found in the cartouche-shaped box, No. 28.

*Cairo No. 62349; Carter No. 269 b.*
*Length 10⅝ in. (27.0 cm.), width*
  *5³⁄₁₆ in. (13.2 cm.), depth 1⁹⁄₁₆ in.*
  *(4.0 cm.).*
*Carter III, 67, 78-9, pl. XXI B;*
  *Desroches-Noblecourt 188, 302,*
  *pl. XL b.*
*Exhibitions: None.*

## 31
## NECKLACE
## WITH LUNAR PECTORAL
## COLOR PLATES 18-19

Pectorals attached to necklaces and decorated with figures of deities or symbols associated with them formed a high proportion of the large amount of jewelry found in Tutankhamun's tomb. This pectoral symbolizes the nocturnal journey of the moon across the sky. At the base is the long, narrow hieroglyphic sign for the sky, appropriately inlaid with blue lapis lazuli. Beneath it are fringe-like inlays of feldspar and lapis lazuli representing drops of moisture; they are added to the sky sign in the hieroglyphic writing of words meaning dew and rain. Lotus flowers and buds grow from the celestial waters and a golden bark seems to be floating above them. This arrangement illustrates the convention regularly adopted by Egyptian artists to show two objects on the same plane when one object was behind the other: the farther object was placed above the nearer. In this case the bark must be understood to be floating on top of the sky sign behind the flowers. To indicate that the bark is conveying the moon and not the sun, the crescent is added to the moon's disk, again in accordance with convention. Furthermore, the moon and crescent are made of electrum, a mixture of silver and gold and therefore lighter in color than pure gold or red carnelian, which were the materials normally used in representations of the sun. The bark itself with its incurved prow and stern is a development in more solid material from the ancient Nile craft made of stems of papyrus lashed together. The design is the same as that of both the sun's bark and the bark used to convey the dead on funerary voyages to the sanctuary of Osiris at Abydos. A thin cord, of which traces can be seen at the base of the moon's disk, is not part of the equipment of the vessel but a simple device for attaching the pectoral to the clothing in order to keep it in position when worn. Its presence suggests that the necklace, like many of the other objects found in the cartouche-shaped box, No. 28, was a personal possession worn by the king in his lifetime.

The chains of the necklace consist of four rows of spherical and barrel-shaped beads made of gold, lapis lazuli, carnelian, feldspar, and resin. Carter considered that the dark-colored resin was perhaps the most remarkable material used in Egyptian jewelry; he was not, however, referring to these beads in particular. At the top of the necklace is a gold cloisonné counterpoise inlaid with a lotus flower and buds, two poppies, and two rosettes. Ten bead tassels, each ending in a faience corolla, are attached to a gold bar supported by the lotus flower. The clasp consists of a tenon that projects from the left-hand corner of the counterpoise and slides into a mortise in the upper terminal bar of the necklace. The lower terminals, which are joined to the pectoral, bear the king's personal name and his throne name, flanked by uraei with outstretched wings embracing the sign of "infinity" (shen).

*Cairo No. 61897; Carter No. 269 k.*
*Length of chains 9¼ in (23.5 cm.), width of pectoral 7¹⁄₁₆ in. (10.8 cm.), width of counterpoise 2⅝ in. (6.8 cm.).*
*Carter III, 76-7, pl. XIX C; Wilkinson 144, pl. LIV B; Aldred, Jewels, 220-1, pl. 101; Vilímková 41.*
*Exhibitions: None.*

## 32
### SCARAB BRACELET
### COLOR PLATE 17

Like Nos. 29-31, this massive gold bracelet was found among the objects placed in the cartouche-shaped box, No. 28, some of which bear evidence suggesting that they were used by the king in his lifetime.

The central feature is a gold openwork scarab encrusted with lapis lazuli. The ancient Egyptians adopted the scarab *(Ateuchus sacer)* as a symbol of the sun god because they were familiar with the sight of the beetle rolling a ball of dung on the ground and this action suggested to them that the invisible power which rolled the sun daily across the sky could be represented pictorially as a scarab. Moreover, they had noticed that the young beetle emerged from a ball of dung by what they imagined to be an autogenic process, so that a further parallel was seen between this creature and the sun god, who was also credited with having created himself. In reality the ball of dung rolled by the scarab is only a reserve supply of food that it hides in a convenient crevice, whereas the ball containing the egg is pear-shaped and is never moved from the burrow in which it is placed by the female. In the Egyptian language the words for the scarab and for existence were identical *(kheper)*, and the name of the sun god, on his first appearance every morning, was Khepri. In hieroglyphic writing the scarab sign was used for all three words.

In spite of black being the color of the scarab in nature, the Egyptians seldom copied it in their reproductions, perhaps because there was no native semiprecious stone of that color, and obsidian, volcanic glass, was not easily obtainable. Quite exceptionally, however, two scarabs placed on Tutankhamun's mummy were made of black resin (see No. 31). Glazed specimens were usually green or light blue, and it is clear that no importance was attached to reproducing an exact likeness of the living beetle. Lapis lazuli, the material used for most of the scarabs in Tutankhamun's collection of jewelry, has not been found in Egypt, the nearest source at present known being Badakhshan in northeast Afghanistan, more than 2,000 miles away.

On each side of this bracelet is a narrow raised band composed of gold, lapis lazuli, turquoise, quartz, and carnelian inlay, bordered on the inner edge with gold granules. The bands are continued on the back of the hoop. Two identical botanical ornaments flank the scarab, each consisting of a mandrake fruit supported by two poppy buds, with gold marguerites filling the interstices between the stems of the mandrake and the buds. The yellow and green

colors of the mandrake are painted at the back of the translucent quartz inlay. Both the hinge and the fastening are made of interlocking cylindrical teeth held together by long gold pins, the hinge pin being fixed and the other movable.

*Cairo No. 62360; Carter No. 269 n.*
*Max. diameter 2⅛ in. (5.4 cm.).*
*Carter III, 77, pl. XX A; Fox 28, pl.*
*48 B; Wilkinson 106, XXIV, pl.*
*XXX A; Aldred, Jewels, 225, pl.*
*110; Vilímková pl. 54.*
*Exhibitions: London No. 35;*
*U.S.S.R. No. 29.*

## 33
### ORNATE PEN HOLDER
### COLOR PLATE 20

The earliest inscriptions written in the hieroglyphic script belong to the beginning of the dynastic period (about 3100 B.C.) and the last known example – an inscription found at the island of Philae – is dated to August 24, A.D. 394. Between those two extremes, the script underwent enormous changes, both in the number of signs employed and in their outward appearance; an inscription can often be dated approximately by the character of its signs. In the time of Tutankhamun about 700 signs were in regular use, but many of them had more than one significance. It is hardly surprising that writing was a professional accomplishment that needed prolonged training for its mastery, nor is it surprising that scribes were a privileged class, having their own patron deity (the ibis-headed god Thoth) and enjoying exemption from paying taxes and doing forced manual work. Besides the hieroglyphic script, they had to learn its cursive derivative, known as hieratic, and, in late times (from about the seventh century B.C.), a derivative of hieratic called demotic.

Scribes in Tutankhamun's time were usually portrayed holding the so-called scribe's palette, a narrow strip of wood or ivory about 9¾ inches (25 cm.) in length with two small cavities at one end and a long, central slot partly open and partly covered, sometimes with a sliding lid. The cavities held solidified ink of two colors, black and red, the former made of carbon and the latter of red ocher, both of which, in their powder form, had been mixed with weak solutions of gum to produce small cake-like blocks when dry. The central slot held the pens, which were really brushes made of short, slender stems of rushes *(Juncus maritimus)*, their tips cut at a slant, like a chisel, and then chewed by the scribe to separate the individual fibers. When writing, the scribe dipped his

*Above: A scribe's palette, the papyrus burnisher (Cat. no. 34), and the pen holder (Cat. no. 33)*

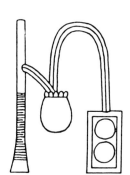

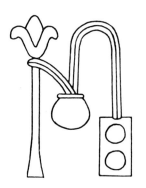

brush in water and rubbed it on the surface of the solidified ink, which quickly dissolved. The true pen, made of a hollow reed *(Phragmites aegyptiaca)*, was used for writing Greek documents in Egypt in the fourth century B.C., but apparently was not used by the Egyptians for writing in their own scripts until Christian times.

Before the combined ink and brush-holder palette was invented, scribes used two separate articles, a smaller rectangular palette with two cavities for the inks, and a tubular case for brushes. An additional item in their equipment was a small bag of leather or linen that contained extra supplies of solid ingredients for making ink. In its earliest form the hieroglyphic sign for a scribe consists of these three articles joined by string, and it is evident that the brush case was a simple reed, closed at the base with a plug (upper drawing). In the course of time the bag was discarded and replaced by a bowl to hold water, and the brush case was made of wood or some other material and shaped like a miniature palm tree. The hieroglyphic sign was accordingly adapted so that it reproduced the water bowl and the brush case in its developed, almost lily-like form (lower drawing).

Tutankhamun provided himself for his next life with a number of composite palettes of the kind described above (one is illustrated at the left) and this very elaborate brush holder. It is made of wood overlaid with chased gold and inlaid with ornamental bands of carnelian, obsidian, and blue and green glass. In form it represents the architectural palm-tree column with a flaring, foliate capital, a rectangular abacus, and disk-shaped base. Both the abacus, which serves as a lid and pivots on a pin, and the base are made of painted ivory. The king's names are engraved in cartouches between the two middle bands of the ornament.

The inclusion of writing equipment in the furniture of the tomb does not imply that Tutankhamun

was able to write. Chapter 94 of the Book of the Dead puts the following words in the mouth of the deceased person: "Bring me the water bowl and [scribe's] palette, which are the writing materials of [the god] Thoth, and the secrets that belong to them." Tutankhamun, by having his own equipment, was merely making sure that he would have, for use in the next world, what he thought the god Thoth required of him.

*Cairo No. 62094; Carter No. 271 e. Height 11 13/16 in. (30.0 cm.), diameter 13/16 in. (2.1 cm.). Carter III, 68, 79-80, pl. XXII D; Desroches-Noblecourt 148, pl. IV b; Fox 28, pl. 40 c; Černý, Paper and Books, 11-30. Exhibitions: None.*

## 34
## PAPYRUS BURNISHER
## COLOR PLATE 20

This handsome object was found with a small group of articles used in writing, one of which was the pen holder (No. 33). Although uncommon, it is not unique, nor is it the only instrument of its kind found in association with the equipment of a scribe. Carter himself discovered a similar tool, but made of wood, with a set of writing implements in a tomb at Thebes, when he was excavating for Lord Carnarvon in the early years of this century, and there are four examples in the Egyptian collection of the Metropolitan Museum, one of which, though incomplete, still bears the name of its owner, the scribe Merymaat. From their shape, it has been deduced that they were used for polishing sheets of papyrus in order to remove slight irregularities on the surface that would hinder the even application of ink.

Papyrus, from which our word paper is derived, was used by the ancient Egyptians from very early times. The oldest written specimens known at present date from the end of the Fifth Dynasty (about 2380 B.C.), but an unwritten roll of material that has been identified as papyrus was found in a First Dynasty tomb (about 3000 B.C.) at Sakkara, and the hieroglyphic sign that probably represents a roll of papyrus was used as early as the First Dynasty.

Sheets of papyrus were made from the stems of a sedge plant (Cyperus papyrus) that, in ancient times, grew in the marshes of Lower Egypt. In the process of manufacture the stems were first cut into pieces of uniform length, generally about 15¾ inches (40 cm.), and the green outer rind was peeled off. The white inner pith of each piece was then divided lengthwise into a number of thin, flat strips, either by slicing it with a knife or again by peeling. When these preparatory stages were finished, some of the strips were laid side by side, perhaps with a fine overlap, on a flat board, followed by a second layer of strips, similarly arranged but superimposed on the first layer and laid at right angles to it. By beating the double layer with a wooden mallet, the sap was released and both the individual strips and the two layers became firmly welded together to form, when dry, a very durable sheet of writing material. If a document was too long for one sheet, additional sheets were pasted together with an adhesive. A burnisher would be particularly useful for smoothing the step in a join of such a kind.

Tutankhamun's burnisher is composed of two pieces, the head and the handle, both of which are made of ivory. The head is capped with gold foil, cushioned on a strip of linen coated with an adhesive on both top and bottom surfaces. It is inscribed with his name and his throne name, coupled with his titles and the regular phrase "Given life like [the sun god] Ra." Carved in one piece with the head is a stylized lily, the corolla of which is shaped to fit the rectangular outline of the head, although the sepals are represented

naturalistically. Unless the yellow appendages are merely decorative, they may be intended to suggest a tie attaching the head to the flower. The slender handle reproduces the thin stem of the lily, here given the appearance of greater strength by the binding at the junction of the flower and the stem. It is evident that such a handle would not withstand the strain imposed on it in use and therefore the burnisher was probably a model intended for funerary purposes. At the base of the handle is a terminal in the form of a papyrus flower.

Cairo No. 62095; Carter No. 271 g.
Length 6½ in. (16.5 cm.), max. width 1¹¹⁄₁₆ in. (4.4 cm.), max. thickness 1³⁄₁₆ in. (2.2 cm.).
Carter III, 81, pl. XXII C; Desroches-Noblecourt 148, pl. 87; Lucas 137-40; Fox 28, pl. 40 B.
Exhibitions: None.

*At the left of this box appears the set of writing equipment as found, wrapped in linen*

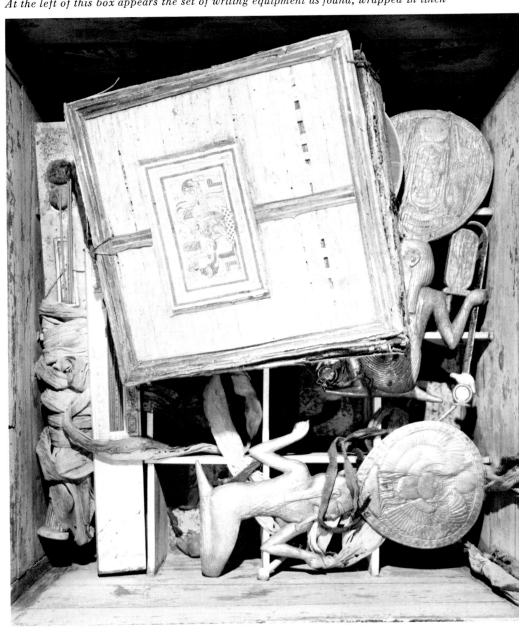

Egyptian sculpture in the round, if it portrays a king or a queen, very seldom shows the subject performing an action, although representations in relief of kings engaged in religious and secular activities are very common (see Nos. 6, 13, 18, and 51). This piece, which shows the king harpooning from a boat made of papyrus stems, is an exception to the rule, and artistically it is an outstanding example of the Egyptian sculptor's ability to represent realistically the poise of the human body at a chosen point in course of movement.

In pharaonic times hippopotami frequented the swamps and papyrus marshes of the lower Nile; even as recently as the beginning of the last century the traveler W. J. Bankes recorded that a hippopotamus had reached the Delta, though at that time it must have been a very exceptional occurrence. Ancient Egyptian nobles hunted them, and representations of such hunts were sometimes included among the wall decorations of tombs. The method employed was to attach a cord to a barb and to project it by means of a harpoon. When several barbs had entered the animal so that it had become weak through loss of blood, it was pulled to the bank by the cords and killed.

Here the king is shown with the harpoon in his right hand and the coil of rope in his left. He is engaged, however, not in an ordinary hippopotamus hunt but in the performance of a religious rite. According to a legend preserved in a late text on a wall of the temple of Edfu, the god Ra-Harakhty when he ruled on earth conducted a military expedition into Nubia accompanied by his son, Horus. While still away from home, he received news that his throne was in danger and he decided to return to Egypt. On reaching Edfu he instructed Horus to attack the enemy, whose identity is not at that point specified, though subsequently reference is made to Seth (the god of evil) and his confederates. Horus carried out his attack by first flying to the sky in the form of the sun's disk with wings and then swooping down on the enemy, killing very many, though a number seem to have escaped. Thinking his victory was complete, he returned to the boat of Ra-Harakhty. The surviving enemies, however, changed themselves into hippopotami and crocodiles in order to attack the sun god in his boat. Once more the battle was taken up by Horus and this time he and his followers slaughtered the enemy with harpoons, pursuing them down the Nile until they were utterly destroyed.

Although the legend — which is not the only one of its kind — had probably undergone many changes in detail by the time it was recorded at Edfu for presentation in the form of drama, the essential features are unlikely to have been very different in the days of Tutankhamun. This figure very probably commemorates such an event, or at least one in the same cycle, with the king impersonating the god Horus, of whom he was thought to be the earthly embodiment. The hippopotamus of Seth would not be shown for magical reasons, because his presence might be a source of danger to the king.

It is one of a pair of similar figures found together in one of the black wooden shrines set against the south wall of the Treasury. Both figures were enveloped in single sheets of linen extending from the shoulders to the ankles. Carved in wood, the figure of the king is coated with gesso and gilded. Its eyes of glass (perhaps with pupils of obsidian) are set in bronze or copper sockets, the same metal being used for the eyebrows. The boat, also made of wood, is painted green apart from the bindings of the papyrus stems and the calices, both of which are

gilded. Beneath the boat is a rectangular wooden pedestal varnished with black resin. The king wears the red crown of Lower Egypt, a bead collar, pleated kilt with apron, and sandals. The uraeus, sandals, harpoon, and rope are made of bronze, all except the rope being gilded.

*Cairo No. 60709; Carter No. 275 c. Height of figure 27⅜ in. (69.5 cm.). Carter III, 54-6, pls. XIII, LX; Desroches-Noblecourt, pls. 159, XLV; Drioton 41, pl. 120; Riesterer pl. 24; Fairman 26-36; Fox pl. 57; Vandier III, 358, pl. CXV, 6.*
*Exhibitions: London No. 27; U.S.S.R. No. 8.*

# 36
# MODEL BOAT
## COLOR PLATE 20

Until the seventeenth century B.C., when the two-horse chariot was brought to Egypt by the Asiatic invaders known as the Hyksos, wheeled vehicles were never used in the Nile Valley. From the earliest times onward, the regular vehicle of transport was the boat. Nature had provided a river that was navigable at all seasons, and sailing against the current was greatly simplified because the prevailing wind blew in that direction, i.e. from the north. In the minds of the Egyptians, travel and ships were so closely linked that the stars and the sun were conceived as moving across the celestial ocean in boats, and every night the sun god was believed to make his perilous journey through the waters of the underworld in his night bark. When an image of a god was taken from its own sanctuary to visit another temple it went by boat, and the boat was carried to and from the quay on poles mounted on the shoulders of priests. The dead too needed boats to travel in the next world. Navigable craft, however, were not necessary; wooden models or even painted representations were considered effective substitutes.

This boat is one of seven of its kind that, together with four other boats equipped with masts, rigging, and square sails, were stacked higgledy-piggledy, mostly on the tops of shrines, in the innermost chamber of Tutankhamun's tomb. Since it has neither oars nor sail, it must have represented a barge that would be towed in a flotilla on some formal occasion. It may have been a model of one of the boats used to transport mourners and furniture to the tomb at the time of the king's funeral, or it may have been intended for his pilgrimage in the afterlife to sacred places such as Abydos and Busiris. Nothing in its build or decoration is truly indicative of its function.

Apart from the yellow and green extensions with their shallow keels at the stem and stern, the hull is carved from a single block of wood, probably acacia. It is shaped in a graceful curve to represent a carvel-built craft suitable for sailing on the Nile. The main deck has been hollowed to a depth of half an inch (1.2 cm.) below the level of the bulwarks. Amidships is an elongated cabin, its stepped roof following the curve of the hull and the walls of both its upper and lower sections terminating at the top in dados and cavetto cornices. In the forecastle and poop are screens for the crew, mounted on decks overhanging the gunwales on both sides. Two long steering paddles are manipulated in upright crutches held firmly at the top by a horizontal bar and fixed at the base to a crossbeam in front of the poop deck. The walls of the screens and the cabin are covered with a multicolored checker pattern broken on the starboard and port sides of the cabin by two doors and three windows in the lower section, and two additional windows in the upper section on the port side. Two green bands and two bands of blue, white, and red concentric circles at the lower ends of the feather pattern on the hull resemble strengthening ties.

*Cairo No. 61339; Carter No. 310. Length 47¼ in. (120.0 cm.), height 8 1/16 in. (20.5 cm.). Carter III, 34, 60-61, pl. III; Desroches-Noblecourt 83.*
*Exhibitions: None.*

Twenty-two black wooden shrines were stored in the innermost room of Tutankhamun's tomb, and each of them contained one or two figures of either the king (see Nos. 35, 38) or a deity. Most of the deities are well known (see No. 39), but some are scarcely mentioned in Egyptian religious literature, and information about their attributes and connections is very slender. To the latter category must be assigned this gilded wooden serpent with eyes of translucent quartz, painted at the back and set in copper or bronze sockets. In spite of the shortness of the tail, it is clearly a cobra with neck dilated like the uraeus on the brow of a king.

An inscription painted in yellow on the black pedestal describes the deceased Tutankhamun as "beloved of Netjer-ankh," which leaves no room for doubt that the name of the serpent deity was Netjer-ankh, meaning the "living god." A serpent with that name, or its variant Ankh-netjer, is represented on painted wooden coffins found in middle Egypt and dating from some five centuries before the time of Tutankhamun; on the underside of its hood is the emblem usually associated with the goddess Neith, a feature also seen on the serpent in Tutankhamun's tomb. The serpent depicted on the coffins is, however, not shown alone but as one of a group of five serpents, all with different names and more than one with the emblem of Neith on its hood. It has been suggested that each of the serpents originally represented one of the mystical elements immanent in the royal uraeus, and thus were minor deities with specialized functions.

In the Eighteenth Dynasty at Thebes the priests of Amun, the national god, endeavored to synthesize the different local conceptions of the afterlife in a book called Am Duat, meaning "What is in the underworld," which describes, with illustrations, the nocturnal journey of the sun god through the underworld from the western to the eastern horizons. The "book" appears, for the first time, on the walls of the tomb of Thutmose III, who died a hundred years before Tutankhamun. It is divided into twelve sections, each representing both one hour of the night and a geographical region, the latter being the subterranean counterpart of an important cult center in Egypt itself. The journey

was fraught with dangers, largely caused by malevolent demons that tried to bar the sun god's progress, but, with the aid of friendly deities and mysterious demigods, he always emerged triumphant on the eastern horizon in the morning. One of the demigods in serpent form, who acted as the custodian of the entrance to the sixth section of the underworld, bears the name Netjer-ankh, who may be the same divine entity as his namesake on the earlier coffins, but to whom the priests of Amun had assigned a different function. This serpent, however, does not bear the emblem of Neith on its hood, although two other serpents, which assist the sun god in the eleventh section of the journey, not only bear the emblem, at least in some representations, but are accompanied by Neith herself (shown in the drawing above). The name is certainly of greater significance than the emblem, but it must be conceded that there is no exact parallel in the Book of Am Duat, or in any other New Kingdom religious work, either to the serpent on the coffins or to Tutankhamun's gilded serpent. Variations in form, in function, or in name are not surprising after so long a lapse of time, and there is little doubt that Tutankhamun's figure represents one of the serpents that he believed would help him in his passage through the underworld, either with the sun god or actually as the sun god himself.

*Cairo No. 60754; Carter No. 283 a.*
*Height 22¼ in. (56.5 cm.).*
*Carter III, 51-3, pl. LIX B; Keimer*
*  "Histoire de serpents" 1 ff., fig. 11;*
*  Jéquier 12-15, figs. 34-38.*
*Exhibitions: None.*

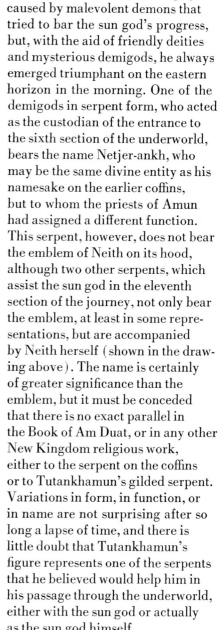

# THE KING UPON A LEOPARD
## COLOR PLATE 21

This composite figure is one of a pair of images shrouded in linen sheets and placed in a single black wooden shrine (illustrated at lower right). It consists of a figure of the king and a figure of a leopard, both mounted on pedestals. Apart from details such as the uraeus and the sandals, which are made of gilded bronze, the whole composition is carved of wood, the figure of the king being coated with gesso and gilded. The eyes and eyebrows are inlaid with glass. Only the facial markings and the internal pectinations of the ears of the leopard are gilded, though traces of gilt are also visible on the claws; the rest of the body is covered with a black resin varnish. The king wears the crown of Upper Egypt, a broad bead collar, pleated kilt in the Amarna style, apron, and sandals, the soles of which are imitated in gilt on the surface of the pedestal. He holds a flail in his right hand and a long staff in his left, his handrest being in the shape of a papyrus flower; both are made of gilded bronze. The name of the king is painted in yellow on his pedestal.

Wooden leopards with mortises cut in their backs, which when complete must have been parts of similar models, were found in the tombs of Amenhotpe II (about 1453-1419 B.C.), Thutmose IV (about 1419-1386 B.C.) — now in the Museum of Fine Arts, Boston — and Haremhab (about 1321-1293 B.C.), but, apart from showing that the Tutankhamun examples were not without parallel in the tomb equipment of kings in the Eighteenth Dynasty, they offer no help in solving the problem of their interpretation. Rather more instructive is a painted representation of a figure of the same general character on a wall in the tomb of Sethy II (about 1199-1193 B.C.), the chief difference being that the statuette of the king and its pedestal are mounted upon a lion. From this slender evidence it may be deduced

that such figures were connected with incidents in the passage of the king through the underworld. The black color of the leopard also suggests a connection with the underworld. It is not a black "panther," in the zoological sense; the underworld was dark and its inhabitants, human, animal, and divine, lived in darkness and were therefore represented in black, the color of darkness. It would have been inappropriate to depict the king in black because he was associated with the source of light, namely the sun god, who passed through the underworld each night, bringing a brief spell of light to its inhabitants.

*Cairo No. 60714; Carter No. 289 b.*
*Height 33 11/16 in. (85.6 cm.), height of king 22 3/16 in. (56.4 cm.), height of leopard 7 5/8 in. (19.4 cm.).*
*Carter III, 56, pl. XIV; Desroches-Noblecourt 249, fig. 158; Bonnet 581-2; Fox 30, pl. 56; Riesterer pl. 24; Vandier III, 359, pl. CXV, 5.*
*Exhibitions: London No. 28; U.S.S.R. No. 9.*

## 39
## THE GOD PTAH
## COLOR PLATE 22

Ptah was the principal god of
Memphis, the capital of Egypt in the
time of the kings who built the
pyramids, and his importance in the
country as a whole must have been
partly a result of his association with
the early seat of government. In
later times Amen-Ra, the god of
Thebes, achieved very wide recognition in a very similar way when
Thebes was the capital. The Greeks
identified Ptah with their god
Hephaistus because he was the patron
deity of artists and craftsmen;
Ptah's high priest bore the title
"Greatest of those who undertake
a craft," or "Chief Artificer."

The theologians of Memphis
maintained that it was Ptah who had
created not only the world but gods,
men, and animals too. In doing so he
was directed by his heart (believed
to be the seat of intelligence), which
prompted his tongue to utter the
name of everything and thereby
bring it into existence. It was a more
intellectual conception of the creation, but less picturesque, than the
notion that the sun god emerged
from the lotus (see No. 1) or, in the
form of a falcon, from an egg,
and it never lost its appeal to the
Egyptians. Other gods were thought
to be immanent in him, merely
members of his body.

This carved wooden figure is
coated with gesso and gilded. Like
many other objects found in the tomb
of Tutankhamun, the gilt on the body,
but not apparently on the face, has
a reddish tinge (see No. 6). The
skullcap is made of dark blue faience
and the eyes and eyebrows are inlaid with glass. A straight artificial
beard of bronze encrusted with gold
is represented as being held in
position by sidestraps. As a rule
figures of Ptah show the god wrapped
in a shroud like a mummy, the head
and hands alone being exposed,
but in this figure the body is wrapped
in a garment of feathers; a broad
collar with back pendant (mankhet)

covers his chest and shoulders.
In his hands he holds a bronze
scepter (was) with an animal head
and the symbols for "life" (ankh)
and "stability" (djed). The figure is
mounted on a pedestal of the same
shape as the hieroglyphic sign for
"truth" (maat) varnished with black
resin and bearing in yellow paint
the inscription: "The good god,
Nebkheperura, son of Ra, Tutankhamun, ruler of Heliopolis of Upper
Egypt, beloved of Ptah, lord of truth,
given life for ever."

*Cairo No. 60739; Carter No. 291 a.
Height of figure 20¾ in. (52.8 cm.).
Pedestal: Length 10³⁄₁₆ in. (26.0
    cm.), height 2⅞ in. (7.4 cm.).
Carter III, 52-3, pl. LV B.
Exhibitions: London No. 6;
    U.S.S.R. No. 6.*

## 40
## MINIATURE EFFIGY
## OF THE KING
## LYING ON A BIER
## COLOR PLATE 23

Carved from a single piece of wood,
this model consists of a figure of
the king wrapped in a shroud and
lying on a bed in the form of two
lions with elongated bodies. Apart
from the hands, which once held the
crook and flail (the insignia of
Osiris), nothing can be seen of his
body except the head and neck on
which the royal *nemes* headdress is
placed. At the sides of the body are
carved almost in the round small
figures of a falcon and a human-
headed bird *(ba)*, each with one wing
laid on the body of the king.

Like so many other objects
from the tomb of Tutankhamun, this
piece has no parallel. It was placed
in a small rectangular wooden sarcophagus padded with linen, and in
this respect, as well as in its general
appearance, it is reminiscent of some
of the *shawabty* figures of its period.
Moreover, a set of miniature implements of the kind made for
*shawabty* figures had been buried
with it. Nevertheless, it is difficult to
believe that it was intended to serve
as an ordinary *shawabty* figure
(see No. 42).

The twin lion bed on which the
figure lies resembles both the bed
used by the embalmers when mummifying the body and the so-called
funerary bed on which it was taken
to the tomb. Tutankhamun's funerary
bed, which was found beneath his
outermost coffin, was made of gilded
wood and its design was very similar
to the pattern of this model. Everything seems to show that the piece
represents in miniature the body of
the king lying on his funerary bed
after the completion of the process
of mummification. The wrappings
and enveloping shroud, which were
held in position by one vertical and
four horizontal bandages, are indicated in this piece by bands of inscription. The human-headed bird and the
falcon are two of the forms that the

king might adopt when visiting his body after it was mummified. A high Egyptian official, who lived not long before the time of Tutankhamun, included in his tomb at Elkab an inscription containing a promise to transform himself into "a phoenix, a swallow, a falcon, or a heron," transformations of a kind also mentioned in the Book of the Dead (cf. Chapters 77-8, 83-6). Chapter 89 has, as its illustration, a representation of the human-headed bird hovering over the body of the deceased that lies on a funerary bed of the same kind as this piece.

The inscription on the central bandage reads: "Words recited by King Nebkheperura [i.e. Tutankhamun]. 'Descend, my mother Nut, spread yourself over me and let me be [one of] the Imperishable Stars that are in you.'" Nut was the goddess of the sky and the Imperishable Stars were the circumpolar stars that did not disappear from view like other stars, but were visible during every season of the year. According to one conception of the afterlife, the dead ascended to the sky and became stars. Understandably they wished to be one of the stars that never died.

The inscriptions on the bier record that the object was the gift of the Superintendent of Building Works in the Necropolis, Royal Scribe, and Superintendent of the Treasury, Maya. It was not his only gift: a fine wooden *shawabty* bears an inscription under the soles of its feet recording that it was "made by the servant who is beneficial to his lord, the Osiris Nebkheperura, the Overseer of the Treasury, Maya." His greatest service to his deceased sovereign, however, may have been rendered in his capacity as "Superintendent of Building Works in the (Royal) Necropolis," an office that would have enabled him to keep an eye on Tutankhamun's tomb after the king's death, and it is possible that it was he who resealed it after the ancient robbers had violated it.

*Cairo No. 60720; Carter No. 331 a.*
*Length 16⅝ in. (42.2 cm.), width 4¹¹⁄₁₆ in. (12 cm.), height of bier 1¹¹⁄₁₆ in. (4.3 cm.).*
*Carter III, 84-6, pl. XXIV; Desroches-Noblecourt 88, 135, 216-9, pl. LIV, 281, 305, fig. 182; Fox 29, pl. 55; Žabkar 84.*
*Exhibitions: Paris No. 34; London No. 10; U.S.S.R. No. 16.*

## 41
## SQUATTING FIGURE
## OF A KING
## COLOR PLATE 16

This figure of solid gold was found, wrapped in a piece of linen, within a gilded miniature coffin. It represents a king wearing the *khepresh* crown (see No. 17) with uraeus and a kilt with the regular apron in front. The upper part of his body, apart from a bead necklace, and his arms and legs below the knee are bare. In his right hand he holds the crook and flail (see No. 5); the left hand rests on his knee. At the back of the neck is a loop for the plaited gold suspension chain. Instead of a clasp, linen cords terminating in tassels are attached to the upper ends of the chain for fastening the necklace.

In addition to this figure, the gilded coffin contained two smaller coffins, one inside the other, the innermost being inscribed with the name of Amenhotpe III's wife, Queen Teye, and preserving a lock of her auburn hair. It has therefore been conjectured that the squatting figure represents Amenhotpe III (about 1386-1349 B.C.), but in the absence of an inscription the identity cannot be proved. Howard Carter regarded the figure and the lock of hair as heirlooms that were buried with Tutankhamun because he was the last successor of Amenhotpe III in the direct line of descent. Other writers have considered them as evidence that Amenhotpe III and Teye were the parents of Tutankhamun. Both the gilded coffin and the outermost wooden coffin, however, bore the names of Tutankhamun, and it seems more probable that the figure represents Tutankhamun himself. In support of this identification is the fact that the lobes of the ears are shown pierced for earrings, a feature seldom shown in representations of kings before Akhenaton (see No. 29).

Egyptian kings and nobles are often shown on monuments wearing necklaces with pendants, and a number of the finest pieces of this kind from the tomb of Tutankhamun are included in this volume. As a rule, however, such pendants were amuletic in character, or at least reproduced mythological events. A squatting king is both exceptional iconographically and difficult to understand in its underlying conception. The pose is at first sight suggestive of the representations of the sun god as a child squatting on a lotus flower (see No. 1), who is also sometimes depicted holding the crook and flail in one hand. The lotus flower was, however, an essential element in the composition of the scene because it provided the support for the sun god when he emerged from Nun, the primordial waters, to bring light to the universe at the time of its creation. In this pendant the king is squatting on a thin plate of gold and, although he is young in appearance, he is clearly not a child. In Egyptian art kings, unless they were engaged in some recognizable activity such as hunting, warfare, or religious ceremonies, were usually portrayed either standing or seated on a throne. Even before the end of the reign of Amenhotpe III, however, conventional styles were undergoing changes, which developed rapidly under Akhenaton and continued, in a more restrained form, under Tutankhamun. It is therefore not improbable that the figure, whether it represents Amenhotpe III or Tutankhamun, is merely an example of the many artistic innovations of the time that possessed no symbolical significance and were soon discarded.

*Cairo No. 60702; Carter No. 320 c.*
*Height 2⅛ in. (5.4 cm.), length of chain 21¼ in. (54 cm.), diameter of chain ⅛ in. (0.3 cm.).*
*Carter III, 86-7, pl. XXV C; Desroches-Noblecourt 134-5, pl. III a.*
*Exhibitions: London No. 46; U.S.S.R. No. 11.*

## 42
## SHAWABTY FIGURE
## COLOR PLATE 23

In the time of Tutankhamun a statuette of this kind was known as a *shawabty*, probably because such figures were originally made of the wood of the persea tree, which was called *shawab* in the Egyptian language. Later the name was changed to *ushabty*, a word meaning "answerer," perhaps because the original connection with *shawab* wood had been forgotten and it fitted the function of the figure as one who answered on behalf of the dead owner. As a rule such figures, even those of kings, were just formal representations of their dead owner, not portraits. In this case the sculptor has produced in wood (cedar?) what seems to be a likeness of Tutankhamun, the lower part of his body being shrouded like a mummy. He is depicted wearing the blue *khepresh* crown (see No. 17) with gilded uraeus and headband. The broad collar and the flail in his right hand are also gilded, but the crook in his left hand is bare. An inscription written in hieratic on one of the boxes containing many of Tutankhamun's *shawabty* figures (this figure was in a black wooden shrine) records that the figures were made of *mry* wood to which gold leaf had been applied, but the word *mry* has not yet been identified.

Shawabty figures are among the commonest objects that have been preserved from ancient Egypt. Some 413 figures of varying quality and material were found in this tomb alone, while the tomb of Sethy I, who reigned about forty years later than Tutankhamun, yielded about 700, by far the highest total from any single tomb. When *shawabtys* were first introduced as part of the equipment of an Egyptian tomb (under the Eleventh-Twelfth Dynasties, about 2000 B.C.), they were very few in number, sometimes only one figure in a tomb. Their number was not substantially augmented until the Eighteenth Dynasty (about 1570-1293 B.C.). In the case of nonroyal persons the ideal number—at least at certain times—was 401, one figure for every day in the year and 36 foremen to control each group of ten figures. The figures were made in the temple workshops under the direction of a priest who bore the title "Chief Fashioner of Amulets," no doubt because the main occupation of his workshop was the manufacture of the small protective amulets that were placed in mummy wrappings and were worn by persons in life. The family of a dead person bought the figures, and the money paid served the dual purpose of paying the vendor and paying the notional wages of the figures.

Although they were sometimes called "servants" in Egyptian texts, *shawabtys* were more often considered as substitutes or deputies for their deceased owner when he was required by the god Osiris to perform corvée duties of an agricultural kind in the next world. This conception underlies the spell from the Book of the Dead (Chapter 6), part of which is inscribed on the front of this figure.

The dead Tutankhamun is represented as addressing the *shawabty* and instructing him that, if he (i.e. Tutankhamun) is summoned to work in the god's domain " to cultivate the fields, to flood the meadows, or to transport the sand of the east to the west," he (i.e. the *shawabty*) shall say that he is ready to do the work for him. The crook and flail are the emblems of the god Osiris (see No. 5) and throughout the text Tutankhamun is identified as the god Osiris.

Incised under the feet is the inscription: "Made by the servant, beloved of his lord, the General of the Army, Minnakht, for his lord, the Osiris, King Nebkheperura, justified." The figure was therefore a gift from the general to the king's funerary equipment.

*Cairo No. 60830; Carter No. 318 a.*
*Height 18⁷⁄₁₆ in. (48.0 cm.).*
*Carter III, 82-3, pls. XXIII,*
    *LXVII; Fox 29, pl. 54; Černý,*
    *Hieratic Inscriptions, 12-13; Schulman 61-6, 68.*
*Exhibitions: None.*

This graceful figure of the goddess Selket, whose emblem, a scorpion, is placed on her head, is made of wood overlaid with gesso and gilded. She is clad in a close-fitting pleated dress with short sleeves, the dress being gathered in at the waist by a ribbed girdle. A pleated shawl, draped over her left shoulder, extends down her back and is knotted under the right breast. Over both garments she wears a broad collar, modeled to imitate rows of beads. Her headdress represents a linen kerchief into which her hair is gathered, tied at the nape of the neck, and continuing downward as a broad flap. The eyes and eyebrows are painted in black.

In its naturalistic style this figure resembles the art of Amarna, but its most striking feature is the turn of the head sideways so that it faces toward the left. It is the more remarkable because it breaks one of the most fundamental and persistent rules of Egyptian plastic art, the so-called rule of frontality. By this rule every figure carved in the round must face the viewer directly. The effect of the deviation in this instance is to show the head in profile, as though it were carved in relief. Amarna influence may be detected in the long neck, as exemplified by the famous head of Nafertiti in Berlin. The outstretched arms and hands are also long, as well as thin, but the reason for this was probably functional, as will be evident when the purpose of the figure is described. Nevertheless, both their positioning and their anatomical character contribute to the piece's elegance as a work of art.

Freestanding figures of four goddesses, one being this figure of Selket, were placed outside the gilded wooden shrine that housed Tutankhamun's alabaster Canopic chest (see Nos. 44, 45). The other three goddesses were Isis, Nephthys, and Neith, each of whom bore, like Selket, her emblem on her head. They were the guardians of the four genii (Imset, Hapi, Qebehsenuef, and Duamutef) with whom the mummified internal organs of the king were identified. Selket was the guardian of Qebehsenuef. All four goddesses had their arms outstretched in the same fashion, such an attitude being suggestive of spreading their protection over their charges. They are represented in high relief with outstretched arms and wings on the corners of both the alabaster Canopic chest and the quartzite sarcophagus

containing Tutankhamun's mummy, and the purpose in each case was the same. An inscription that refers to similar figures on the sarcophagus of Thutmose IV defines their role in these words: "These four goddesses shall be with you, accompanying you, driving out every evil that is in your flesh, exterminating those who come against you and setting their magic spells against them." The sideways glance of the three goddesses who faced the sides and back of the shrine, Selket, Neith, and Nephthys, was also intended to suggest that they were looking out for intruders.

Selket's divine role was not limited to funerary duties; like her three companion goddesses she acquired those functions in virtue of her long-established reputation in a wider field of protection. Childbirth and nursing were two human activities with which she was associated, but she was chiefly noted for her control of magic and, in particular, for treating scorpion stings by means of magic. It may seem strange that a goddess whose emblem was a scorpion should be concerned with nullifying its actions, but homoeopathy — the countering of like by like — played an important part in ancient magic; no doubt she was believed to have at her command the particular poison contained in the sting of a scorpion and could use it for therapeutic purposes. Professional magicians are often mentioned in Egyptian texts as being attached in a priestly capacity to the cult of Selket, perhaps as specialists in curing scorpion stings. A well-known magical papyrus in the Turin Museum ascribes the following words to one of these magicians: "It is not I who utter it [i.e. a spell], it is not I who repeat it; it is Selket who utters it, it is she who repeats it." The magician in this instance claimed to be no more than the mouthpiece of the goddess, a feature of priesthood that is not uncommon. With the exception of Isis, no Egyptian goddess was more closely connected with magic than Selket, and even Isis sometimes assumed the form of a scorpion or was represented as being escorted by scorpions and thereby identified herself with Selket.

*Cairo No. 60686; Carter No. 266 a.*
*Height 53⅝ in. (90 cm.).*
*Carter III, 46-51, pls. V, VIII; Desroches-Noblecourt 78, 83, 85, pl. XXXI; Piankoff 19-20, pl. 12; Yoyotte 128, pl. 129; Bonnet 696-7.*
*Exhibitions: None.*

*Left: The shrine containing Tutankhamun's Canopic equipment. Above: Three of the goddesses who surrounded the shrine; Selket (Cat. no. 43) is at the right*

## 44
## STOPPER
## FROM CANOPIC CHEST
## COLOR PLATE 12

The gold miniature coffin (No. 45) containing one of the king's internal organs, perhaps the lungs, was placed in one of four cylindrical compartments in a magnificent Canopic chest shaped like a shrine. It was covered by a linen pall and placed on a gilded wooden sledge (see No. 43). The whole chest, except the movable lid, was carved of a single block of alabaster (calcite). On the outer walls were inscribed magical utterances by four goddesses, depicted at the four corners with their arms outstretched, namely Isis, Nephthys, Selket, and Neith. They were the protectors of the Four Sons of Horus (Imset, Hapi, Qebehsenuef, and Duamutef), with whom the internal organs were identified. At the top of each of the inner compartments was a stopper, made of alabaster, in the form of the head and shoulders of a king wearing the striped royal headdress with the vulture's head and the cobra separately carved and inserted in the brow. Details of the features are picked out in black and red. The likeness to Tutankhamun is so striking that it is hard to imagine that the sculptor was not portraying the king himself. Each stopper has a black symbol on the shoulder to indicate the particular compartment into which it fitted.

Although chests containing the deceased's mummified viscera are known as Canopic chests, the name has no historical justification. Usually such chests held four jars, the actual receptacles of the viscera, which, until shortly after the time of Tutankhamun, were provided with human-headed stoppers. Later, one stopper only was human-headed and

three represented heads of a baboon, a jackal, and a falcon, the forms ascribed to the Four Sons of Horus. Canopus was the name given by the Greeks to a town near Alexandria after one of their legendary heroes, Canopus, the pilot of Menelaus, perhaps because they believed he was buried there. It was the seat of a cult of Osiris in which the god was represented as a bulbous jar with a human head, not unlike the jars used for preserving the viscera. Once the town had acquired its name, it is not difficult to understand how ancient visitors to Egypt imagined that it was Canopus himself, and not Osiris, who was worshiped in the form of a human-headed jar. Early European antiquarians, unaware of the difference between the Osiris jars and the human-headed jars that contained the viscera, added to the error of the ancients by associating the viscera jars with Canopus and calling them Canopic jars, a name they have retained to this day.

*Cairo No. 60687; Carter No. 266 e.*
*Height 9⁷⁄₁₆ in. (24 cm.), max. depth*
  *7⁷⁄₁₆ in. (19 cm.).*
*Carter III, 46-50, pls. IX, X, LIII;*
  *Desroches-Noblecourt 78, 83, 161,*
  *pl. XXXIII, 222, 238, 246, 301;*
  *Fox 27, pls. 44-5; Aldred, Art,*
  *89, pl. 147.*
*Exhibitions: U.S.A. No. 24; Paris*
  *No. 30; Japan No. 15; London*
  *No. 8; U.S.S.R. No. 13.*

## 45
## CANOPIC COFFIN
## COLOR PLATES 26-27

This is one of four miniature coffins, all of the same form but differing in their inscriptions, which were placed in an alabaster (calcite) chest, the so-called Canopic chest (see No. 44). They are made of beaten gold, inlaid with colored glass and carnelian. Each coffin contained one of the internal organs of the king — liver, stomach (or spleen), lungs, and intestines — that were removed from his body during the process of embalming. In design these coffins are miniature replicas of the second of the three anthropoid coffins within which the king's mummy was placed.

Tutankhamun's names in the inscriptions appear to have been substituted for others that have been completely erased. It may therefore be conjectured that the coffins, like some of the other objects in the tomb, were originally made for Smenkhkara, Akhenaton's co-regent at the end of his reign. This explanation would account for the general facial resemblance to Tutankhamun if, as seems probable, the two kings were brothers.

The mummiform effigy is portrayed wearing the striped royal headdress *(nemes)*, with the vulture's head and the cobra on the brow, a plaited beard on the chin, and an elaborate collar composed of imitations of petals. The lobes of the ears are pierced for earrings after the fashion of the period. Crossed over the chest and held in each hand are the shepherd's crook and the flail (see No. 5), emblems of the god Osiris with whom the dead king was identified. Two vultures, one with the head of a cobra representing the goddess Wadjet and the other representing the goddess Nekhbet, spread their wings over the arms and shoulders of the effigy; they hold in their claws the hieroglyphic sign for "infinity" *(shen)*. The lower part of the body is decorated in cloisonné work with a stylized feather pattern arranged in compartments. In the center of the front, inlaid in colored glass, is the inscription: "Words spoken by Selket: 'I place my arms on that which is in me, I protect Qebehsenuef who is in me, Qebehsenuef of the Osiris, King Nebkheperura [i.e. Tutankhamun], justified.'" The goddess Selket, on the underside of the lid (illustrated at the right), is shown standing on the hieroglyphic sign for "gold" and enveloping with her wings a packet

containing one of the internal organs, perhaps the intestines. The remainder of the inside of the lid and the whole of the inside of the box are covered with magical inscriptions.

*Cairo No. 60691; Carter No. 266 g. Length 8⅞ in. (22.5 cm.).*

*Carter III, 46-51, pls. LIII, LIV; Desroches-Noblecourt 83, 162, pl. XXXIV, 220, 222, 301; Fox 27, pl. 46; Piankoff 19, pl. 9.*
*Exhibitions: Similar to U.S.A. No. 2; Paris No. 31; Japan No. 2; London No. 9; U.S.S.R. No. 12; Vienna No. 58.*

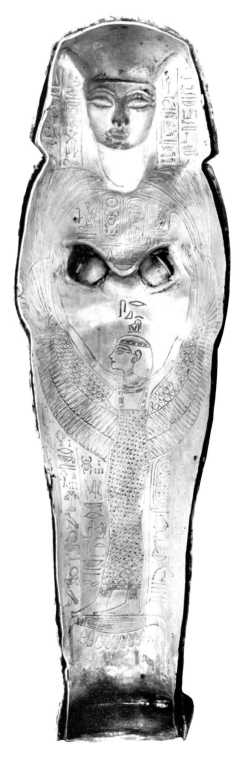

157

In the introduction to Chapter 17 of the Book of the Dead, playing a game called *senet* is described as one of the occupations of the deceased person in the next world, and the vignette accompanying the chapter represents him seated, often in the company of his wife, at a checkerboard but without an opponent. Like so many other activities ascribed to the next life, playing this game was also something that the deceased had done in his lifetime. It must have a long history, because it is represented occasionally in the scenes on the walls of Old Kingdom tombs, a thousand years before the time of Tutankhamun, sometimes in association with music and other kinds of entertainment. On the standard board there were generally three rows of ten squares, five of which might be inscribed with hieroglyphics; each player had five or seven playing pieces, frequently conical in shape.

To judge from the number of boards in Tutankhamun's tomb, the game must have been one of his favorite pastimes. The boards – four in all – vary in size from a miniature set to the largest and most elegant, which is shown here. It is box-shaped and is mounted in a rebate on top of an ebony stand in the form of a bed frame with feline paws resting on gilded drums. Beneath the drums is an ebony sledge. The claws of each paw are made of ivory and the "cushions" and the braces, which strengthen the joints between the frame and the paws, are gilded. The box itself is veneered with ebony and the thirty squares, five of which are inscribed, are inlaid with ivory. At one end of the board is a small drawer for the gaming pieces. Originally it was fastened by two bolts, probably of gold, which slid into staples fixed on the frame. Since the pieces were missing, Carter supposed that they were made of gold and silver and were stolen by the ancient robbers.

Like many of the other known examples, this box is double-sided, the game played on the reverse side being called *tjau*, a word that seems to mean "robbers." That board is divided into twenty squares, a middle row of twelve squares flanked by four squares on each side at one end. Three of the squares in the middle row are inscribed, one with a kneeling figure of Heh, the god of millions of years, another with two thrones in pavilions (the sign for a jubilee festival), and the third with the hieroglyphic signs for life, stability, and dominion.

Nothing is known with certainty about the rules of play for either game, but it is believed that the aim of each player in *senet* was to be the first to reach the square at the angle of the L-shaped arrangement inscribed with three signs meaning "happiness, beauty." The square preceding it may have been a hazard, because its hieroglyphs represent water. Certainly it was a game of chance, the moves being determined by the throw either of knucklebones or of four casting sticks, both of which were found in the tomb. The casting sticks were of two kinds, one pair having ends in the form of the tips of human fingers and the ends of the other being carved in the form of a long-eared canine animal, probably a fox. Both pairs consist of black ebony in the upper half and white ivory in the lower half. Perhaps the number of points scored from a cast depended on the number of sticks that finished with the white or black side uppermost when they were cast.

Besides the reference in the Book of the Dead to the game of *senet*, another religious text mentions what appears to be the same, or at least a very similar, game played by the deceased against a divine opponent to decide his fate in the underworld. The extant versions of this text all date from later than the time of Tutankhamun, but they may preserve an ancient belief. Nothing, however, in the character of his boards suggests that they were

specially intended for religious or funerary purposes. The incised inscriptions filled with yellow pigment on the sides and ends of this box are strictly mundane, wishing the king life and prosperity and employing such titles and epithets as "The Strong Bull, beautiful of birth, image of Ra, precious offspring [literally "egg"] of Atum, king of Upper and Lower Egypt, ruler of the nine bows [i.e. foreign lands], lord of all the lands, and possessor of might Nebkheperura." On the other side he is called "Fair of laws, he who pacifies the Two Lands, 'the Horus of Gold' exalted of crowns who placates the gods." The short inscriptions around the drawer, which are of the same kind, describe him as "The good

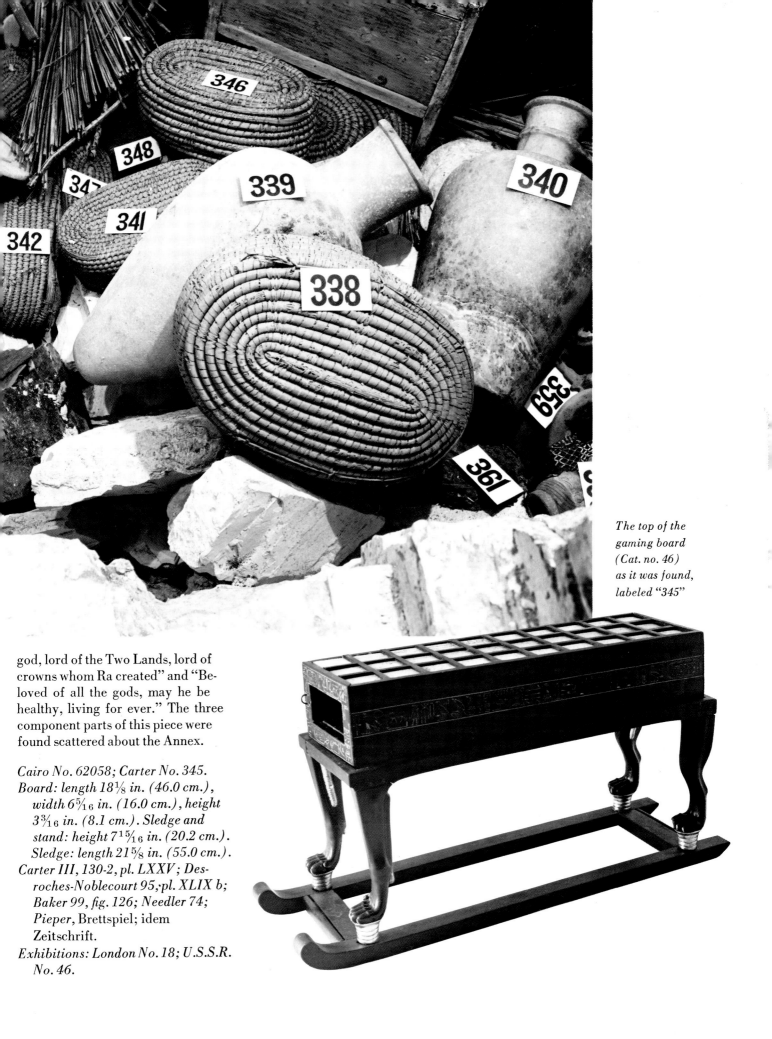

*The top of the gaming board (Cat. no. 46) as it was found, labeled "345"*

god, lord of the Two Lands, lord of crowns whom Ra created" and "Beloved of all the gods, may he be healthy, living for ever." The three component parts of this piece were found scattered about the Annex.

*Cairo No. 62058; Carter No. 345.*
*Board: length 18⅛ in. (46.0 cm.),*
*    width 6⁵⁄₁₆ in. (16.0 cm.), height*
*    3³⁄₁₆ in. (8.1 cm.). Sledge and*
*    stand: height 7¹⁵⁄₁₆ in. (20.2 cm.).*
*    Sledge: length 21⅝ in. (55.0 cm.).*
*Carter III, 130-2, pl. LXXV; Des-*
*    roches-Noblecourt 95,; pl. XLIX b;*
*    Baker 99, fig. 126; Needler 74;*
*    Pieper, Brettspiel; idem*
*    Zeitschrift.*
*Exhibitions: London No. 18; U.S.S.R.*
*    No. 46.*

## 47
## ALABASTER FLASK
## COLOR PLATE 30

Finely carved stone vessels were one of the outstanding achievements of the early Egyptian craftsmen. Making use of the rich variety of materials available to them, they produced vases and dishes of a quality and simple elegance that were never surpassed and seldom equaled in later times. Basalt, breccia, diorite, schist, and alabaster were the stones most commonly employed, serpentine and granite not infrequently, particularly in the early dynastic period, and rock crystal and porphyry exceptionally. Many thousands of vessels of these materials were buried with King Djoser (about 2650 B.C.) under his famous step pyramid at Sakkara, and very large numbers were placed in tombs of nobles and high officials at the beginning of Egypt's history. After the Old Kingdom (about 2180 B.C.) the production of stone vessels, apart from small unguent pots in the Middle Kingdom, diminished until the middle of the Eighteenth Dynasty, when there was a notable revival. New and more elaborate shapes were designed and the material employed was generally native alabaster, a stone that should strictly be described as calcite.

This flask is one of a pair of almost identical vases fashioned in a new style and apparently not in large numbers, to judge from the known examples. It is made of the finest alabaster, with no break in the continuity of the gentle curves of its outline. Spaced apart on its long neck are three inlaid bands of imitation lotus petals, the blue being faience and the white limestone, all suspended from strings of black and white glass. They represent the garlands that were regularly at this period attached to pottery jars at feasts and were reproduced, as characteristic features, on painted pottery at the palace of Amenhotpe III and at Amarna. Stains on the alabaster suggest that the vase had been used in the king's lifetime; the slight residue of its contents remaining inside the vase could not be identified.

*Cairo No. 62129; Carter No. 344.*
*Height 26¹⁄₁₆ in. (66.2 cm.), diameter 7¹¹⁄₁₆ in. (19.6 cm.).*
*Carter III, 147, pl. LXXXIX B; Desroches-Noblecourt 188, pl. XL a, 302.*
*Exhibitions: U.S.A. No. 23; Japan No. 16.*

## 48
## HEADREST
## COLOR PLATE 29

Egyptian headrests show many variations in material, and in form they range from the plain to the elaborate. Usually they consist of three parts: a flat base, a small central pillar, and a curved support on which the head rested. In this ivory example, which has no close parallel in Egyptian art, the central pillar is formed mainly of a figure of the god Shu kneeling and holding with upraised arms the curved head support. Looped over each of his shoulders is the hieroglyphic sign for "protection." Two couchant lions, carved almost in the round, are on the top of the base.

Shu was the god of the air and consequently his image was used as its symbol. According to legend he brought chaos to an end, at the creation of the universe, by raising the sky (symbolized by his daughter Nut) high above the earth (symbolized by his son Geb). It was an action that had to be maintained continuously; failure to do so would result in the fall of the sky and a return to chaos.

The ancient Egyptians regarded the head as the seat of life and consequently its preservation was thought to be of particular importance for continued existence after death. It could not, however, function without the help of magic, which could be obtained by various means, one of which was an amulet in the form of a headrest, either model or actual. Tutankhamun possessed four full-size headrests and one model that was made of iron and placed in the linen wrappings of his mummy at the back of the head — the natural position for such an object. A spell in the Book of the Dead (No. 166) has been interpreted as attributing to the headrest the power of resurrection, and another spell (No. 55) sometimes written on headrests identifies these objects with the god Shu, probably because air was a vital necessity for life.

In order to show symbolically that the base of the headrest represents the earth or its god Geb, the artist has carved two lions, one at each end of the base, representing the two mountains on the eastern and western horizons between which the sun rose and set. As a development from this conception, two squatting lions placed back to back became a symbol for yesterday and tomorrow. On the shoulder of each lion is a kind of rosette, the interpretation of which is uncertain. It has been variously explained as representing a tuft of hair and an ornament placed on live lions at the court of a king. Its occurrence as an artistic feature is not confined to Egypt; it is also found in the art of Syria, Mesopotamia, and Persia. The position of the tail, lying beside the body, is a peculiarity of the period (see No. 16). At other times it was curled over the flank.

Behind the figure of Shu is the hieroglyphic inscription: "The good god, son of Amun, king of Upper and Lower Egypt, lord of the Two Lands, Nebkheperura [i.e. Tutankhamun], given life like Ra for ever."

The object is made of two pieces of ivory joined by a wooden dowel in the middle of the figure of Shu and held together by four gold nails. Details are inlaid with a blue pigment.

*Cairo No. 62020; Carter No. 403 c.*
*Height 6⅞ in. (17.5 cm.), length 11⁷⁄₁₆ in. (29.1 cm.), width 3½ in. (9.0 cm.).*
*Carter III, 116-7, pl. XXXVI B; Desroches-Noblecourt 288, pl. 187; Fox 31, pl. 62; Piankoff pl. 59.*
*Exhibitions: Paris No. 41; London No. 37; U.S.S.R. No. 39.*

## 49
## ORNATE STOOL
## COLOR PLATE 31

Egyptian stools fall into two main classes, folding and rigid. Within each class there is a wide variety of patterns, ranging from the simple to the elaborate, many of which are represented in the furniture found in the tomb of Tutankhamun. A fine model of a folding stool is included here (No. 11) and two illustrations of the king seated on such a stool with a cushion may be seen on the sides of the gold shrine (No. 13). In a third scene, on the left-hand door of the same shrine, he is shown seated on a rigid stool that is also covered with a cushion. A fine distinction cannot be drawn between the different uses of stools and chairs in ancient Egypt, but in the time of Tutankhamun chairs are more common in representations of formal occasions and stools in scenes of the ordinary activities of daily life.

The wood of which this stool is made has not been identified with certainty, but it is believed to be acacia, one of the very few kinds of timber grown in Egypt that were suitable for furniture. It is painted white apart from the grille, stretchers, feet, and cartilaginous protuberances on the legs, all of which are gilded. Under the feet, the ringed drums are capped with metal, either copper or bronze. The double-cove seat is bordered on the outer edges by a narrow cornice, which contributes to the lightness and elegance of the piece. It is the gilded grille, however, which is the most distinctive feature of the stool. On all four sides it consists of the hieroglyphic sign for "unification" *(sema)*, to which are tied stems of the lotus and papyrus flowers. It is a motif regularly found on the sides of the seats in royal monuments, sometimes with figures of two deities, representing Upper and Lower Egypt, holding the ends of the stems. As a symbol it commemorated the unification of the Two Lands (i.e. Upper and Lower Egypt) under Menes, the first king of the First Dynasty (see No. 10). In ancient times the papyrus plant flourished in the marshes of the Delta, and the artist has suggested this natural setting by showing the stems of the flowers emerging from a row of leaves at the base. The corresponding feature at the base of the lotus stems represents a plot of land divided by irrigation channels, the canals being the natural habitat of the lotus in Upper Egypt. As a hieroglyphic sign it is sometimes used to indicate the general sense of the Egyptian word for Upper Egypt *(shema)*. The stretchers under the grille are decorated with the striated design found on the borders of the inner gilded panels of the chair illustrated as No. 8.

In one respect this stool, apart from being a seat, resembles a chair: the front and the back are easily distinguishable, the front being the face corresponding with the direction in which the feline feet are pointed. In decoration there is no difference between the two faces, except that the lotus and papyrus flowers are on opposite sides of the *sema* sign and therefore back to back. This arrangement shows that the stool was intended to be placed facing eastward, so that the papyrus would be on the northern side and the lotus on the southern side.

Although it is solidly built, with

mortise and tenon joints strengthened by metal pegs capped with gold, it has suffered some distortion from the strain of being tightly wedged between a bedstead and the wall of the Annex, where it had been thrown by the ancient robbers in their hurried operations in the tomb.

*Cairo No. 62038; Carter No. 467.*
*Height 17¹¹⁄₁₆ in. (45.0 cm.), width 17¹¹⁄₁₆ in. (45.0 cm.), depth 16¹⁵⁄₁₆ in. (43.0 cm.).*
*Carter III, 114, pl. LXVIII B; Baker 87, pl. VIII; Desroches-Noblecourt 93, pl. IV a.*
*Exhibitions: Paris No. 14; London No. 20; U.S.S.R. No. 44.*

# 50
# POMEGRANATE VASE
# COLOR PLATE 30

Egypt, so rich in gold, had very little native silver. It did, however, possess, though not in very large quantities, a natural alloy of gold and silver, electrum, which was so light in color that it was sometimes called "white gold." Early texts that mention both gold and silver place silver first, which suggests that it was the more valuable metal, but the order had been reversed by the Eighteenth Dynasty, when an appreciable amount of silver must have reached the country from western Asia as tribute and in trade. Nevertheless, it was not common; the tomb of Tutankhamun yielded only two "silver" objects of any size – this vase and one of the two trumpets (see No. 3) – but probably some other pieces had been stolen by the ancient robbers. Alfred Lucas, the chemist who assisted Carter, noted that this vase contained "a considerable proportion of gold and might be regarded as either silver or electrum."

Whether the material of which the vase is made came from a native source (which seems likely) or not, the pomegranate whose fruit it imitates was certainly not indigenous to Egypt. It was brought from western Asia after the campaigns of the warrior kings of the early Eighteenth Dynasty. Although it is mentioned by its Semitic name, which the Egyptians retained, in a biographical inscription dating from Amenhotpe I or Thutmose I, the earliest representation occurs in the so-called botanical garden of Thutmose III at Karnak – a small chamber whose walls are decorated with reliefs showing the trees and plants that he collected in Palestine and Syria. Thereafter it appears in painted scenes on the walls of the tombs of nobles and high officials, but at first only rarely, in small quantities, and exclusively in the tombs of the most important courtiers. In a tomb at Amarna pomegranate trees are shown growing in the royal garden.

Very soon after the introduction of the pomegranate into Egypt, imitations of it were made in glass and faience (and certainly in other materials too) for use as vases and, in miniature, as pendants to necklaces. Some faience examples were found in the tomb of Thutmose III's son, Amenhotpe II, at Thebes, a circumstance that would be consonant with the assumption that they were a prized novelty. Perhaps more indicative of the esteem in which they were held is a record in the diplomatic correspondence – the so-called Amarna letters – between Tutankhamun's predecessor, Akhenaton, and the king of Babylonia, Burnaburiash, that Akhenaton had sent Burnaburiash a present of silver and ivory pomegranates. In another letter in the same collection of letters Tushratta, king of Mitanni, stated that he was sending Akhenaton seven gold pomegranates. It is evident, therefore, that in the time of Tutankhamun the pomegranate was still uncommon enough for its shape to attract interest. Besides this silver vase, Tutankhamun had an ivory pomegranate, found in the alabaster casket, No. 9.

Chased on the neck and shoulder of the vase are bands of petals. A third band on the body of the vase is composed of cornflowers and leaves, which may be those of a vine, but their identity has not been firmly established. On the neck are nine sepals (one broken in antiquity), whereas in nature the sepals number only five to seven – perhaps an indication that the silversmith who made it was not very familiar with the fruit itself. Originally it had a rush stopper that had been forced into the vase by the ancient robbers in order to obtain whatever it contained.

*Cairo No. 62192; Carter No. 469.*
*Height 5¼ in. (13.4 cm.), diameter 4¼ in. (10.8 cm.).*
*Carter III, 130, pl. LXXIII A; Fox 33, pl. 68.*
*Exhibitions: None.*

Both artistically and technically this wooden chest is undoubtedly one of the outstanding works of art in the whole collection of objects found in the tomb of Tutankhamun. No more than four pieces, of which two are this chest and the small golden shrine (No. 13), show the king and queen together, in a style reminiscent of so much of the art of the preceding Amarna period, but different in theme. Perhaps the most striking difference is that Akhenaton and Nafertiti are generally represented participating almost as equal partners in the performance of some activity, whereas the role of Ankhesenamun tends to be rather subservient, that of an intimate companion who attends to Tutankhamun's needs. The relationship between king and queen is nearer to that of a nobleman and his wife as portrayed in some of the painted tombs of the pre-Amarna period at Thebes, but it is not identical because the nobleman's wife is represented merely as an onlooker.

In its design the chest embodies the main architectural elements of the standard Egyptian cabin-shaped shrine, except insofar as the main dimension is horizontal and not vertical. The lid is an elongated adaptation of the hunchbacked roof. The entablature of the box consists of a cavetto cornice overlaid with gilded gesso and edged with ebony, a wooden torus molding painted dark green, and a narrow ebony frieze. On the ledge above the cornice is an inlaid band consisting of red and blue plaques, the former of painted calcite and the latter of glazed composition, arranged alternately and separated by black and white striped plaques, apparently made of ebony and ivory. A similar band of decoration serves as a border to the painted scenes carved on the lid and in ivory panels on the outer faces of the four walls, each scene being set within a frame composed of broad strips of plain

ivory. The feet are capped with ferrules of bronze or copper.

The difference already mentioned in portraying the relationship between the king and queen in the time of Akhenaton, on the one hand, and Tutankhamun, on the other, is well illustrated in the delightful scene carved in low relief on the central panel of the lid (Color Plate 33). It is set in a bower richly bedecked with flowers, mostly in festoons. The posts supporting the vine-covered roof are decorated with circular floral frills, spaced at intervals apart, open poppies arranged in spiral fashion, and, at the top, clusters of papyrus, lotus, and poppies. Under the bower, the king, leaning lightly with one hand on a long staff, is in the act of stretching out the other hand to receive two bouquets of lotus, papyrus, and poppies from the queen. In contrast with the relaxed pose of the king, her bearing is erect and yet graceful and mobile. Her headdress, surmounted by a conical unguent holder flanked by two uraei with solar disks, is turned toward the viewer, as if it were seen from the front, whereas her head is shown in profile revealing a very long side lock — a feature of coiffure that was a recent innovation. Both the lie of the side lock and the flowing ends of the long sash, which gathers her pleated robe in at the waist, add to the impression of movement in her whole body. She is the devoted and intimate companion of the king, seeking to give him pleasure, but nevertheless ministering to him. Beneath this scene and, in accordance with Egyptian artistic convention, nearer to the viewer (see No. 31), are two female attendants picking flowers and mandrake fruits to take to the king and queen, perhaps when sitting on the cushioned seat with a floral valance reaching to the floor, placed under the bower behind the royal pair.

In virtue of its position and also

The ornate chest and its cover (Cat. no. 51) are numbered "551" and "540" here, amid the confusion of the Annex

of its character, the principal scene on the box is undoubtedly the one carved in low relief on the panel at the head end of the chest (illustrated at right), which depicts Tutankhamun shooting with bow and arrow wild fowl and fish from the bank of a rectangular pond. In accordance with a common artistic convention, part of the string of the bow and the butt end of the arrow are concealed behind the king's head and body, while his right hand, which holds them, is shown in the position it would occupy if the string were on the near side of his head (cf., however, Nos. 13 and 18). His extended left arm is protected by an archer's leather bracer from injury through friction caused by the string. He is seated on a curved-back chair with a cushion, and his feet rest on a cushioned footstool. He wears the blue crown with uraeus and pendent streamers, a broad bead collar, and a pleated skirt tied around the waist by a long sash, the ends of which reach nearly to the ground, and an apron also suspended from the waist. On his arms and wrists are broad bracelets and on his feet sandals. The lobe of his ear is pierced for an earring (see No. 29). The queen squats on a cushion in front of the king holding a lotus flower in her right hand and an arrow, ready to pass to the king, in her left hand. Her dress is the same as on the lid. At the top of her wig is a fillet with uraeus and pendent streamers, surmounted by a diadem of uraei with sun's disks. Resting on the wig is a conical unguent holder adorned with a floral circlet. The name and titles of the king (who bore the epithet "beloved of Ptah, Lord of Truth") and those of the queen are engraved in the hieroglyphic inscriptions in front of their figures. Beneath the pond is an attendant carrying a fish and a duck, both transpierced by one of the king's arrows.

As a background to this scene, the artist has filled the entire field with festoons, garlands, and bouquets in which the flowers and individual petals of the blue lily, buds of the white lotus, and the leaves and fruit of the mandrake are predominant. Among other plants recognizable by their flowers and leaves are convolvulus, cornflowers, and possibly a vine. Even the gap between the legs of the king's chair and the narrow aperture between the stiles and the backrest are draped with flowers. Two upright bouquets, each surmounted

by a lily palmette and a blue lotus and supporting buds of red poppy, stand one at each side of the panel, giving the appearance of architectural columns and suggesting to the eye that the action is taking place under a bower. The whole composition is intended to convey the impression of the idyllic surroundings in which the king would lead his afterlife.

Very similar floral motifs are repeated on the sides and back of the chest, but their setting is entirely different. Each panel has, within its ribbon border, a frieze consisting of

*Right side:* a spotted calf rising to its feet, an ibex attacked by a lion, a spotted bull in flight, two spotted calves, one recumbent, the other running, a spotted calf in flight with its hind legs in the air.

Just as the scene on the lid resembles some of the episodes on the gold shrine (No. 13), so these scenes have much in common with those on the reverse side of the sheath of the gold dagger (No. 20), and it is not inconceivable that in both cases they were drawn by the same draughtsman or at least by draughtsmen from the same workshop. At first sight those on the box appear to have little connection with the scene on the front panel, but the hound is clearly the royal hunting animal and, although the king himself is not shown, the whole composition gives the impression of being the hunting counterpart to the fowling and fishing scene, in which it was necessary to represent the king as the archer whose arrows secured the prey.

Although this chest had been stripped of its contents by the ancient robbers and had been separated from its lid, so that the box was found in the northwest corner of the Annex and the lid in the northeast corner, it may be deduced that it probably held some of the king's ceremonial robes. It was fastened by a string tied round the gilded wooden knobs on the lid and the head end of the box, the knot being sealed.

*Cairo No. 61477; Carter No. 540 (lid), 551 (box).*
*Length 28⁵⁄₁₆ in. (72.0 cm.), width 20⁷⁄₁₆ in. (53.0 cm.).*
*Carter III, 118, frontispiece; Baker, 95-7, fig. 117; Desroches-Noblecourt 95, pl. 176; Fox 32-3, pl. 65; Harris 39, pl. 35; Yoyotte 125.*
*Exhibitions: Paris No. 24; London No. 21; U.S.S.R. No. 48 (all without lid).*

a black and white checkered band and white pendent petals on a blue and red background above a rectangular black and white frame, which is divided by three oblique wavy lines, colored black, red, and black, into five compartments on each side and two compartments at the end. Within these compartments are representations of animals, some being attacked by other animals and others without visible attackers. It is noticeable that the legs of the animals often cut across the dividing lines, but the floral backgrounds are kept inside the divisions. Beginning from the end with the panel already described, the following episodes are shown:

*Left side:* a spotted calf attacked by a white hound wearing a collar, an ibex in flight, a spotted calf in flight, a spotted bull attacked by a cheetah that has jumped on its back, and an ibex attacked by a white hound wearing a collar.

*Back, right:* an ibex attacked by a cheetah that has leaped on its back; left: a spotted bull attacked by a hound wearing a collar.

## 52
## ROYAL SCEPTER
## COLOR PLATE 31

This scepter is made of sheet gold beaten on a wooden core. The shaft is in the form of a papyrus flower and stem; it is embellished at each end with a feather design in cloisonné work inlaid with carnelian, turquoise, lapis lazuli, feldspar, faience, and glass. Embossed on one side of the blade (illustrated at the left) are rows of trussed and slaughtered bulls, partly dismembered, beneath a frieze of lotus petals between borders of checker and diamond patterns. On the other side of the blade, beneath a similar frieze, is an inscription reading: "The good god, the beloved, dazzling of face like the Aton when it shines, the son of Amun, Neb-kheperura, living for ever."

Scepters of this kind have three names in Egyptian texts, *kherep*, "the controller," *sekhem*, "the powerful," and *aba*, "the commander." They were carried as symbols of authority from very early times, but no distinction can be drawn between their various uses. In temple ritual and in the mortuary service the *aba* scepter was often held by the officiant who presented the offerings. If the sacrificial offerings shown on the blade of this scepter are indicative of its use, it probably represents the *aba* scepter, but precise identification is not possible. It was found in the Annex, whither it had probably been taken from the Treasury by the robbers.

*Cairo No. 61759; Carter No. 577.*
*Length 21¼ in. (54 cm.), width*
*2⁹⁄₁₆ in. (6.6 cm.).*
*Carter III, 133-4, pl. XLIV; Des-*
*roches-Noblecourt 202, pl. 123;*
*Fox 33, pl. 67.*
*Exhibitions: London No. 38;*
*U.S.S.R. No. 19.*

## 53
## STANDING LION JAR
## COLOR PLATE 28

This alabaster (calcite) unguent jar is carved in the form of a lion standing upright on a pedestal, the head and body being hollowed out to hold the unguent. The teeth and the tongue are made of ivory, the latter stained red; the eyes are gilded. The left front paw rests on the hieroglyphic symbol for "protection," while the right is held high. Both front paws have holes for the insertion of claws, perhaps made of ivory. The right back paw, slightly raised, is placed in advance of the left, a pose that differs from that of standing figures of men, in which the left leg is generally forward. Fixed to the top of the lion's head is a crown-like addition that serves as the mouth of the vase. It consists of a circular base from which project representations of pointed sepals of the blue lotus and single lilies surmounted by single papyrus flowers and small rosettes. Tufts of hair, inlaid with blue pigment, are engraved on the back of each shoulder (see No. 48). The lobes of the ears are pierced to hold earrings. On the chest are inscribed the names and titles of Tutankhamun and Ankhesenamun. Beneath the checker pattern band of blue, black, white, and yellow rectangles, the frieze of the pedestal consists of representations of individual lotus petals and mandrakes. The sides of the pedestal are designed in the fashion of trellis-work.

Another alabaster unguent vase found in the tomb of Tutankhamun (No. 16 in this book) is furnished with a lid on which is carved a recumbent lion; two miniature lotus columns on the outside of the vase are surmounted by heads of the god Bes, a domestic deity associated with pleasures of every kind. Egyptian unguent vases frequently embodied in their composition a figure of Bes, usually represented as a bandy-legged dwarf with ears, mane, and tail of a lion. The association of the god with

both the lion and unguent vases is thus very close, and it seems evident that the lion form was chosen for this vase because of the animal's connection with Bes and consequently with receptacles for unguents.

When the vase was found the crown was missing, having been wrenched off by the ancient thieves. The contents, however — some dried fatty substance black in color (see Nos. 10 and 16) — remained intact.

*Cairo No. 62114; Carter No. 579.*
*Height 20⅝ in. (60 cm.), width 7¾ in. (19.8 cm.).*
*Carter III, 144, 146, pl. XLVIII; Desroches-Noblecourt 96; Riesterer pl. 35.*
*Exhibitions: Paris No. 35; London No. 4; U.S.S.R. No. 42.*

## 54
## IBEX VASE
## COLOR PLATE 32

Ivory, stone, and pottery vessels in the shape of animals and birds were made in predynastic times and in the early dynastic period (about 3000 B.C.), but subsequently they seem to have gone out of fashion until the Eighteenth Dynasty, when, perhaps under western Asiatic influences, their manufacture in stone, pottery, faience, and glass was resumed. As a rule the creatures chosen for this purpose were not those sacred to deities, the ibex being no exception in this respect. Apart from the present example it occurs in painted representations of vessels in the tomb of a high official of the Eighteenth Dynasty named Kenamun and in a relief dating from the time of Thutmose III in the temple of Karnak. As an ornamental motif the head and neck were sometimes fixed on the outside of vases near the rim. They are also reproduced in the round as figureheads on the prow and stern of an alabaster boat found in Tutankhamun's tomb.

The most distinctive features of the ibex *(capra nubiana F. Cuvier)* are usually its long, curved horns and a short beard. In this vase (and also in the figurehead on the stern of the boat) the beard has been broken off. Only one of the horns has survived; it is a real horn of the animal and not an imitation. The attachment of real horns to models of animal heads was not an innovation of the Eighteenth

Dynasty; bulls' heads made of sun-baked clay and provided with real horns were sometimes mounted on low platforms in niches in the outer walls of tombs of the First Dynasty. Both the body of this ibex and the pedestal on which it rests are carved of a single block of alabaster (calcite), but the ears and tail are made of separate pieces. The tongue, projecting from the mouth and suggesting

that the animal is bleating, is made of ivory stained red. Paint has been used for the eyes, which are overlaid with glass and set in copper or bronze sockets, for the markings on the head, and for the cartouche (see No. 28) on the left shoulder, which bears Tutankhamun's throne name, Neb-kheperura, surmounted by the sun's disk and plumes.

In the center of the back is an

orifice into which a low funnel with flat rim was probably inserted. If the funnel was covered with a stone cap fixed with cement, it would explain why the ancient robbers, when stealing the oil from the hollowed-out body of the animal, found it simpler to wrench off the whole funnel than to remove merely the lid. Their action in emptying the vase when so much gold lay within their reach shows how valuable its cosmetic contents must have been.

*Cairo No. 62122; Carter No. 584.*
*Length 15⅛ in. (38.5 cm.), width*
*   7⁹⁄₁₆ in. (18.5 cm.), height 10¹³⁄₁₆*
*   in. (27.5 cm.).*
*Carter III, 147, pl. XLIX B; Des-*
*   roches-Noblecourt 212, pl. XLIV,*
*   303.*
*Exhibitions: None.*

## 55
## COMPOSITE BOW
## COLOR PLATE 28

In the intricacy of its decoration this angular bow is one of the most elaborate of some fifty weapons of its class found in Tutankhamun's tomb. It is composed of a thin wooden stave overlaid on both faces with a middle layer of a gelatinous substance (perhaps decayed sinew) that has been molded on the inner face to form a keel, and an outer layer of tree bark (possibly birch). Both the "back" and the "face" are ornamented symmetrically on each side of the grip with geometric, chevron, and floral motifs inlaid and bordered with gold,

gold granulations, and gold bands. The pattern is broken on the "face" by clumps of papyrus in flower and on the "back" by figures of an ibex and a horse. Both animals are represented in association with flowers, which are difficult to identify. Perhaps the flowers with the ibex — a desert animal — are some species of desert plant, while the two clumps shown beneath the horse may be lotus. Ostrich plumes adorn the horse's head-stall and an ostrich-plume fan is shown behind its flank (see No. 18).

This bow was found enclosed in a wooden box containing articles of clothing, sticks, and arrows, the mixture probably being the result of the robbers' activities. As a weapon, the simple bow was used by the Egyptians in predynastic times and throughout their history, but the composite bow, of which this is an example, was not introduced until about three centuries before the time of Tutankhamun, when it was brought to Egypt by immigrants from Asia, known as the Hyksos. With it they also brought the horse-drawn chariot, and it was probably the possession of these two advanced weapons that first enabled them to subjugate the Egyptian people. By gumming a sinew to a simple bow, the elasticity of the stave was greatly increased and its range was thereby considerably extended.

*Cairo No. 61518; Carter No. 596 q.*
*Length 40⁹⁄₁₆ in. (103.0 cm.), width*
*   ⅞ in. (2.3 cm.), thickness ⅜ in.*
*   (1.0 cm.).*
*Carter I, 114; McLeod 25, No. 27.*
*Exhibitions: Paris No. 22; London*
*   No. 49; U.S.S.R. No. 22.*

# BIBLIOGRAPHY

ALDRED, C.
*Jewels of the Pharaohs.* London, 1971.
*New Kingdom Art in Ancient Egypt.*
London, 1951.

BAKER, H. S.
*Furniture in the Ancient World.*
*Origins and Evolution, 3100-475 B.C.*
London, 1966.

BONNET, H.
*Reallexikon der ägyptischen Religions-*
*geschichte.* Berlin, 1952.

BOSSE-GRIFFITHS, K.
"The Great Enchantress in the Little
Golden Shrine of Tut'ankhamūn."
*Journal of Egyptian Archaeology.* Vol.
59 (1973), 100-8.

CARTER, H.
*The Tomb of Tut-Ankh-Amen.* 3 vols.
(Vol. I with A. C. Mace.) London,
1923-33.

ČERNY, J.
*Hieratic Inscriptions from the Tomb of*
*Tut'ankhamūn. (Tut'ankhamun's Tomb*
*Series II.)* Oxford, 1965.
*The Valley of the Kings.* Cairo, 1973.
*Paper and Books in Ancient Egypt.*
London, 1952.

DAVIES, N. DE G.
*Two Ramesside Tombs at Thebes.*
New York, 1927.

DESROCHES-NOBLECOURT, C.
*Life and Death of a Pharaoh,*
*Tutankhamen.* London, 1963.

DRIOTON, E.
*Le Musée du Caire. (Encyclopédie*
*photographique de l'art.* Ed. Tel.)
[Paris], 1949.

FAIRMAN, H. W.
"The Myth of Horus at Edfu," *The*
*Journal of Egyptian Archaeology.* Vol.
21, 26-36.

FOX, P.
*Tutankhamun's Treasure.* London,
1951.

GARDINER, A. H.
"Tut'ankhamun's Gold Dagger,"
*Journal of Egyptian Archaeology.* Vol.
27 (1941), 1 (Frontispiece).

HARRIS, J. R.
*Egyptian Art.* London, 1966.

HAYES, W. C.
*The Scepter of Egypt.* Vol. II.
Cambridge, Mass., 1959.

HICKMAN, H.
*La trompette dans l'Égypte ancienne*
*(Supplément aux Annales du Service*
*des Antiquités de l'Égypte,* Cahier
No. I). Cairo, 1946.

JEQUIER, G.
*Les frises d'objets des sarcophages du*
*Moyen Empire.* Cairo, 1921.

KEIMER, L.
"Egyptian Formal Bouquets (Bouquets
Montés)." *The American Journal of*
*Semitic Languages and Literatures.*
Vol. XLI (1925), 145-161.
"Histoire de serpents dans l'Égypte
ancienne et moderne." *Mémoires de*
*l'Institut d'Égypte.* Vol. 50.

LANGE, K., AND HIRMER, M.
*Egypt—Architecture. Sculpture.*
*Painting.* London, 1968.

LUCAS, A.
*Ancient Egyptian Materials and*
*Industries* (4th edition, revised and
enlarged by J. R. Harris). London,
1962.

LYTHGOE, A. M.
"Excavations at the South Pyramid of
Lisht in 1914." *Ancient Egypt,* 1915,
147-53.

McLEOD, W.
*Composite Bows from the Tomb of*
*Tut'ankhamūn (Tut'ankhamūn's Tomb*
*Series III).* Oxford, 1970.

MÖLLER, G.
*Die Metallkunst der alten Ägypter.*
Berlin, 1924.

MORENZ, S.
*Egyptian Religion.* London, 1973.

MORENZ, S., AND SCHUBERT, J.
*Der Gott auf der Blume.* Ascona, 1954.

NEEDLER, W.
"A Thirty-square Draught Board in the
Royal Ontario Museum." *Journal of*
*Egyptian Archaeology.* Vol. 39 (1953),
60-75.

NEWBERRY, P. E.
"The Shepherd's Crook and the so-
called 'Flail' or 'Scourge' of Osiris."
*Journal of Egyptian Archaeology.* Vol.
15 (1929), 84-94.

NIMS, C. F.
*Thebes of the Pharaohs.* London, 1965.

PIANKOFF, A.
*The Shrines of Tut-ankh-Amon.*

Bollingen Series XL. 2. New York,
1955.

PIEPER, M.
*Das Brettspiel der alten Ägypter und*
*seine Bedeutung für den ägyptischen*
*Totenkult.* Berlin, 1909.
"Ein Text über das ägyptische Brett-
spiel." *Zeitschrift für ägyptische*
*Sprache.* Vol. 66 (1931), 16-33.

QUIBELL, J. E.
*Excavations at Saqqara* (1911-12), *The*
*Tomb of Hesy.* Cairo, 1913.

RIESTERER, P. P.
*Egyptian Museum Cairo. The Funeral*
*Treasure of Tutankhamen.* Zurich,
1966.

SCAMUZZI, E.
*Museo Egizio di Torino.* Turin, 1963.

SCHAEFFER, C.F.-A
*Ugaritica* II (*Mission de Ras Shamra,*
Tome V). Paris, 1949.

SCHULMAN, A. R.
"The Berlin 'Trauerrelief' (No. 12411)
and Some Officials of Tut'ankhamūn
and Ay." *Journal of the American*
*Research Center in Egypt.* Vol. IV
(1965), 55-68.

SINGER, C., HOLMYARD, E. J.
AND HALL, A. R.
*A History of Technology.* Vol. I, Ch.
25, "Fine Wood-Work" by Cyril
Aldred. Oxford, 1955.

TAIT, G. A. D.
"The Egyptian Relief Chalice." *Journal*
*of Egyptian Archaeology.* Vol. 49
(1963) 93-139.

VANDIER, J.
*Manuel d'archéologie égyptienne.* Vol.
III, *Les Grandes Époques: La Statuaire.*
Tomes 1 et 2. Paris, 1958.

VILIMKOVA, M.,
ABDUL-RAHMAN, M. H.
AND DARBOIS, D.
*Egyptian Jewellery.* London, 1969.

WILKINSON, A.
*Ancient Egyptian Jewellery.* London,
1971.

YOYOTTE, J.
*Treasures of the Pharaohs.* Geneva,
1968.

ŽABKAR, L. V.
*A Study of the Ba Concept in Ancient*
*Egyptian Texts.* Chicago, 1968.